Adapting
THE LITURGY

Creative Ideas
for the
Church Year

RESOURCE PUBLICATIONS, INC. • San Jose, California

Editorial director: Kenneth Guentert
Production Editor: Elizabeth J. Asborno
Art director: Ron Niewald
Back cover photo: Sandy Underwood

Resource Publications, Inc.
160 E. Virginia Street, Suite 290
San Jose, CA 95112-5848

Library of Congress Cataloging in Publication Data

Marchal, Michael, 1944-
    Adapting the liturgy : creative ideas for the church year /
Michael Marchal.
    p.   cm.
  Includes index.
  ISBN 0-89390-139-3
  1. Catholic Church—Liturgy. 2. Catholic
Church—Liturgy—Texts. 3. Church year. I. Title.
BX1970.M29 1989
264'.02—dc20   89-10241

5 4 3 2 1
93 92 91 90 89

To my sister Mary Caroline
Sis felix nostrumque leves quemcumque laborem.
Aeneid I. 330

Contents

PART ONE
Festival Seasons

Winter Cycle

Spring Cycle

PART TWO
Rites of Initiation for Roman Catholic Children

PART THREE
Special Celebrations

Acknowledgments

Permission was granted to reprint from the following copyrighted material:

First portion of "A Bidding Prayer: Contemporary", *The Book of Occasional Services,* p. 37, and "Litany of Healing," *The Book of Occasional Services,* pp. 148-9. Copyright The Church Pension Fund. Used with permission.

Formula for the "Reception of the Vows of Marriage," *The Book of Common Prayer.* Copyright The Church Pension Fund. Used with permission.

Genesis 3:12-15; Isaiah 7:10-14; Matthew 25:23-25; John 13:12-13; 1 Corinthians 15:55; 2 Corinthians 3:6; Revelation 21:5, excerpted from *The Jerusalem Bible,* copyright 1966 Darton, Longman & Todd, Ltd. and Doubleday, a division of Bantam, Doubleday, Dell Publishing Group, Inc. Reprinted with permission. Taken from *The Jerusalem Bible.* Published and copyright 1966, 1967, and 1968 by Darton, Longman, and Todd, Ltd. and Doubleday & Co., Inc. Used by permission of the publishers.

Hebrews 12:2. Excerpt from *The New Jerusalem Bible.* 1985 Copyright 1966 by Darton, Longman & Todd, Ltd. and Doubleday, a division of Bantam, Doubleday, Dell Publishing Group, Inc. Reprinted with

Throughout this book, I use the abbreviations PC and ACC. They stand for Principal Celebrant, usually a priest or presbyter, and Assisting Concelebrant, either a priest or deacon.

If the ACC is a priest, he and the PC might divide between them the rites' prayers and blessings.

If the ACC is a deacon, he would not usually proclaim prayers or blessings. Instead he proclaims admonitions and invitations and leads certain litanies.

NOTE: None of the adapted rites described in this work are approved for liturgical use.

Introduction

To Liberate Our Worship

At gatherings of Catholic liturgists, one of the common remarks for years has been: How do we get people to do what is in the book? How do we get musicians to sing the liturgy—the responsorial psalm, the Sanctus, and the other acclamations—rather than four hymns that parallel the liturgy? How do we get real symbols into the hands of the congregation, such as eating *and* drinking at Mass, rather than wafers and a sanitary dip in the cup (at the most)? Where do we find clergy who do not begin Christmas Midnight Mass and a wedding and all other Masses with the Confiteor but are comfortable with the options built into the service?

The Order of Mass is an amazing resource, flexible enough to guide the worship of thousands gathered in a stadium or of two or three around a dining room table. Yet so many of its resources do not seem to be common property among American Roman Catholics.

1

How deeply many liturgists experience this divorce between theory and practice recently became clear to me. At a regional meeting, I suggested that membership on worship commissions and the renewal of clerical faculties should be contingent upon an annual exam covering the *General Instruction on the Roman Missal.* Though I meant the remark humorously, a number of those in the room seemed to be nodding in serious agreement.

All that such an academic hurdle would guarantee, though, is more good rubricists, and we know too well what Paul meant by those who try to fit life into laws. Good liturgists are much like directors. They know that the printed text and stage directions are only the beginning. Real liturgy, like real theater, happens when word and gesture and object, when what is heard and done and seen, all work together. Translating the theory of the *General Instruction* into weekly parish worship has been the dream of liturgists for more than two decades.

Yet liturgists are not caretakers of a museum. Turning the 11 a.m. Sunday Eucharist into a duplicate of a fifth-century service is not the dream. Helping modern worshipers to find the same accessibility, the same involvement, the same sense of celebration as our ancient forebears, might be.

To continue the analogy, liturgists are like directors who are trying to stage Shakespeare. How do we make the perennial tales of love and hate, honor and treachery, come alive today? The text is in print; the director must make a myriad of coherent decisions about cuts, costuming, historical setting, sets, music, and more if he or she is to create a valid interpretation still faithful to the original.

For years my seniors have first read *Romeo and Juliet* and then seen Zefferelli's movie version. Their usual reaction is that they are watching a different play from the one they have read. They are partially right but basically quite wrong. Details might be altered, but the spirit of the original is gloriously present. If there were more time, watching *West Side Story* might make that point clearer to them.

Liturgists need a similar freedom. While remaining faithful to the Roman Rite, we must adapt to the resources and the experiences of our real-life worshipping communities. We must stretch and bend a bit, omit and reshuffle and rewrite—without losing sight of our responsibility to maintain our rich tradition and the integrity of the Gospel message. It is a precarious but necessary task if the dream of liturgical renewal is ever to be achieved. "The written letters bring death; the Spirit gives life" (2 Corinthians 3:6).

This book is an attempt to share the results of my experiences of just such adaptation. Both in parish and in school communities I have been fortunate in knowing countless people who have given of their time and talents to making the different celebrations of the liturgical year come alive.

These suggestions are offered to the proverbial "ordinary" parish. They presume only minimal resources. Lectors who can proclaim a text, a few competent musicians and one good leader of song, and a community that is comfortable with (and hungers for) involving themselves in liturgy with their voices and their actions—these are all that is needed to make the resources work. Further musical or artistic enhancement is easy, but only the most basic talents of music, movement, and good taste are required.

To Enhance the Introductory and Communion Rites

One of the great liberations of Vatican II was the radical opening of the Eucharistic liturgy to the ownership of all Roman Catholic worshipers. From being a clerical preserve bound by complex rules, the Mass was to become once again marked by the active participation of all the baptized. The visible consequences were obvious: vernacular texts, altars facing toward the congregation, communion under both species. The auditory consequences were equally momentous: new texts and styles (the "guitar" Mass), spontaneous Prayers of the Faithful, even "on the spot" Eucharistic Prayers.

Much of this outpouring of change and experimentation was necessary: the officially available resources were often meager. Much of it was clearly prompted by the Spirit as Catholics struggled to rediscover how to express the heritage of their faith in their own language, in contemporary words and media. Perhaps the major unfinished liturgical task now is to sort out and assimilate this outpouring into a coherent tradition.

For creativity is not going to go away. The revised Order of Mass is filled with options and with permission to create more options. Other than the three set presidential prayers, the Eucharistic Prayer, the Lord's Prayer, and certain communal songs, the rest of the service can be composed by those celebrating it. Aside from the Free Church tradition, few other denominations officially allow such a wide latitude for public prayer.

We can be proud of this liturgical liberation. Yet a candid observer of contemporary American Catholic worship would see little sign of its presence. Rote performance and repetitive recitation are still too common among laity and clergy. Among the many possible factors that have led to this situation, I would like to propose three for consideration, along with some ways in which renewal might be achieved.

First, the core component of liturgy is prayer. Unless we consciously enter into the presence of that Holy Mystery in which we live every moment, liturgy is not being true to itself. Aesthetically or emotionally the performance may be both quality and very satisfying, but it is not liturgy. Relaxation, togetherness, even chatting have a place at worship, but so do awe and wonder and praise. True liturgy lives at the meeting point of the horizontal and the vertical.

The first way I know to achieve this balance is through architecture. We need at last to take seriously the mandate of the decree *Holy Communion and Worship of the Eucharist Outside Mass* 9, and *physically* separate the tabernacle from the worship space of the assembly. The last vestige of that piety that treated the tabernacle with the etiquette accorded an absolute monarch should be gone from the liturgy. Then we can set about rediscovering and celebrating the unfolding presence of Jesus in the community and its presider, in the Word and the common Meal. After twenty-five years, it is time not just to rearrange the furniture but to seriously redecorate.

Second, there is a need among liturgy planners and performers for a sense of proportion. What works in a retreat house, a small group liturgy, or even in the side chapel on Tuesday morning will not automatically work in the church on Sunday morning, and vice-versa. Large groups do not preclude a sense of community or of individual ownership, but the techniques that produce those qualities are very different. Neither do small groups guarantee intimacy, especially if the participants have come to *watch* the presider do his thing.

The essential prerequisite for achieving successful proportion is a conscious use of space and ritual. Especially in spaces meant for large groups, architectural planners must avoid building theatrical stages with outsized accouterments. I have been in churches where every detail of the structure said that what was up front was what counted—not what was going on in the pews. The ritual in such spaces also tends to be highly visual and minister-centered. Restraint in the size and furnishings of the sanctuary, a significant use of processions, and an active involvement of the community in gestures can draw a whole church (building and people) into a genuine, united experience in the presence of the Holy One.

Third, even if we have a space and a ritual in accord with the liberation of Vatican II, in the actual celebration of worship we tend to make a fatal error: we confuse creativity with spontaneity. We have not accepted the wisdom that any poet or musician or craftworker (even my mother who loved to knit) could have taught us: making art involves discipline, concentration, and attention to detail. In liturgy too there is no substitute for preparation and practice. Improvisation is a skill that develops only *after* training.

We do usually demand a minimal competence of musicians and readers; but how many general intercessions have been the homily outline interspersed with "Lord, hear our prayer!" rather than a thoughtful, sensitive articulation of the needs of the community and the world placed before God? Here and at the introductory rite and the invitation to communion and elsewhere, real creativity means composition and revision and all the other skills of a committed writer.

Let us examine various examples of such creativity.

The first accompanying text is an example of troped Kyries for the introductory rite. The only way out of the confusion that the final revisers of the Order of Mass left in this portion of the Eucharist is the use of the troped Kyrie as a simple and straightforward introduction. The repertoire created for the American sacramentary provides a great variety suitable for diverse seasonal and daily use and is easily expandable.

These tropes need not be proclaimed by the presiding clergy nor need they be merely read. The trope can be read with a leader of song introducing the communal "Lord, have mercy!" or "Kyrie, eleison!," even in a small weekday celebration. (Better a strong introductory set of acclamations than two or even one verse of an "opening hymn.")

In a large assembly, one of the ways to bring the gathering together is frequently to give everyone a simple acclamation to sing. In this way they begin to feel each other's presence and faith. The accompanying texts for the three great festivals of the winter cycle are therefore more musically elaborate (to mark the service as special) and founded upon communal singing of the simplest Gregorian Kyrie, which keeps us in touch with our tradition.

The Christmas tropes are based upon the titles given to Jesus in the Isaiah and Luke readings of Midnight Mass. The Epiphany tropes are more generic, but the Baptism tropes address Jesus in words taken from the various gospel accounts. Rather than a "downer" to begin a festival ("For the times that…"), these tropes in an actual service provide an effective meditative bridge between the triumphant opening hymn and the collective prayer. (The Gloria seems almost redundant.) Similar compositions for other celebrations could be a moment of prayer created by the collaboration of the professional musician and a singing congregation.

CHRISTMAS

Lord Je - sus Christ You are the shin - ing light given to those who walk in
the land of dark - ness Ky - ri - e e - le - i - son Ky - ri - e e - le - i - son

Lord Je - sus Christ You are the won - der coun - se - lor, the God - he - ro, the Prince of peace
Chri - ste e - le - i - son Chri - ste e - le - i - son, Lord Je - sus Christ You are the Good
News to all peo - ple of good will, the sav - ior born to all the world, our Mess - i - ah,
our God. Ky - ri - e e - le - i - son Ky - ri - e e - le - i - son.

Introduction

EPIPHANY

Lord Je - sus Christ migh - ty king be - come a child Ky - ri - e e - le - i -
son Ky - ri - e e - le - i - son Lord Je - sus Christ e - ter - nal King of
jus - tice Chri - te e - le - i - son Chri - te e - le - i - son Lord Je -
sus Christ Light and glo - ry for all na - tions Ky - ri - e e -
le - i - son Ky - ri - e e - le - i - son

THE BAPTISM OF THE LORD

Cantor
Lord Je - sus Christ be - lov - ed Son on whom the Father's fa - vor rests

Congregation   Cantor
Ky - ri - e e - le - i - son. Ky - ri - e e - le - i - son Lord Je -

sus Christ God's cho - sen one on whom the Spir - it de - scends

Congregation   Cantor
and rests: Chri - ste e - le - i - son, Chri - ste e - li - i - son Lord

Je - sus Christ You baptize all who be - lieve in You with the Ho - ly Spir - it

Congregation
and with fire Ky - ri - e e - le - i - son Ky - ri - e e - le - i - son

© 1985 Thomas Miles

11

Another place where tropes are becoming common is the Agnus Dei. With communion under both species and a real fraction as a regular part of the Eucharist, there is a need to restore this invocation to its original litany format. This need has been met by several composers, among them Marty Haugen in his *Mass of Creation,* and David Clark Isele in *Lead Me, Guide Me.*

The accompanying texts are examples taken from Holy Week. Intended for use on Palm Sunday, Holy Thursday, and Easter Vigil, certain titles are repeated for continuity's sake, and others are varied for the specific celebration. Shorter than Kyrie tropes, they can charge an often dull moment in the service with expectation by their almost mantra-like effect.

PALM SUNDAY

Jesus, Blessed One...
Jesus, Humble Lord...
Jesus, Crucified King...
Jesus, Glorious Hope...
Jesus, Cup of Life...
Jesus, Living Bread...

HOLY THURSDAY

Jesus, Perfect Love...
Jesus, Giver of Peace...
Jesus, Humble Lord...
Jesus, Crucified King...
Jesus, Cup of Life
Jesus, Living Bread...

EASTER VIGIL

Jesus, Risen Lord...
Jesus, Paschal Lamb...
Jesus, Living Bread...
Jesus, Wine of Joy...
Jesus, Source of Life...
Jesus, Bond of Love...

When the communion invitation has been written to add a spoken presidential conclusion to the litany, a real sense of continuity in prayer is created.

A portion of the communion rite that is invariant in the Roman tradition is the embolism, the expansion upon the Lord's Prayer that leads into the communal acclamation, "For the kingdom...." In some Western traditions, the Mozarabic Rite of Spain, for example, this prayer *is* variable and shows us how we might extend our tradition in a new direction.

The accompanying texts show how the Holy Week liturgies can be further adapted according to this model.

PALM SUNDAY: The Lord's Prayer

PC: God is with us at every step of life's journey.
Let us turn to him with confidence
and pray together as Jesus taught us:

ALL: Our Father...

PC:
Deliver us, Father, from all that is evil:
from giving in to our weakness and hesitation,
to turning back on the road to Jerusalem

and to life in you.
Give us the gift of your peace,
and keep us free from doubt and anxiety,
as we wait, joyful, in hope,
for the full, final coming of your kingdom.

All: For the kingdom...

HOLY THURSDAY: The Lord's Prayer

PC: One in love and service,
one in prayer as Jesus taught us, let us sing:

ALL: Our Father...

PC:
Deliver us, Father, from every evil
and set us truly free.
Drive out whatever blocks Jesus's coming to us.
May his service bring us your kingdom;
may his weakness bring us your power;
may his Cross bring us your glory,
as we wait with longing and hope
for the full coming of Jesus among us, your people.

ALL: For the kingdom...

EASTER VIGIL: The Lord's Prayer

PC: United by baptism with Jesus, our risen Lord,
let us pray together as He has taught us:

ALL: Our Father...

PC:
Deliver us, Father, from every evil:
from darkness, from smallness of heart.

In your mercy keep us free from sin;
keep us faithful to our alleluias,
as we wait, joyful in hope,
for the full, final coming
of our risen and triumphant Lord, Jesus Christ.

ALL: For the kingdom...

The need for another prayer for peace could thus be eliminated. The current prayer with its address to Jesus is very strange and originated as a private prayer of the priest, becoming communal only in the last revision of the Order of Mass.

Bringing together all of these elements into a continuous whole would allow us to unify the often isolated components of the Communion Rite. Rather than jumping from one action to another, interspersed with private prayers said aloud, the rite can be a gracious and prayerful preparation and sharing of a common meal. The following is an example of a unified rite for Christmas Midnight Mass. While reading it, we must also visualize the gestures and actions that accompany the words, yet also be conscious of the words that are omitted.

CHRISTMAS MIDNIGHT MASS: THE COMMUNION RITE

The Lord's Prayer and Exchange of Peace

PC:
In Jesus, God has called us back
and united our lives with his own life.
With great confidence, then,
let us pray together
as our Brother, Jesus, has taught us:

ALL: Our Father...

PC:
Deliver us, Father, from all that is evil:
from dread and darkness and despair.
Keep us faithful in proclaiming
Your tidings of great joy and peace among us.
Keep us joyful in your Spirit
as we await the glorious return
of our Lord and Savior Jesus Christ.

ALL: For the kingdom...

PC:
At Jesus's birth the angels sang:
  Glory to God in the highest,
    and peace to his people on earth!
  May God's peace come to us now
  and to our whole world.
  May the peace of the Lord be with you!

ALL: And also with you!

ACC/PC: Let us now exchange peace with one another.

The Agnus Dei Litany

Jesus, God's own Son...
Jesus, born of Mary...
Jesus, Word-made-flesh...
Jesus, Life for all...
Jesus, Source of joy...
Jesus, Giver of peace...

The Invitation to Communion

PC:
For us a Child is born;
to us the Son is given.
Among us the Word has been made flesh
and dwells forevermore.
Happy are we who are called to this banquet
to share his glory, his life!

ALL: Lord, I am not worthy....

Communion Song

Postcommunion (Sacramentary)

PC:
God, our Father,
we rejoice in the birth of our Savior.
May we share his life completely
by living as he has taught us.
We ask this in the name of Jesus the Lord.

ALL: Amen.

PART ONE
Festival Seasons

WINTER CYCLE

Advent

> Repent; change your hearts! The kingdom of
> God is right at hand!

For modern American liturgical Christians, Advent is a difficult season to celebrate. On the concrete level of music and decorations, the world of retail avidly celebrates Christmas for at least two weeks before Advent even begins. All around us the world daily becomes more festive just when liturgical tradition calls us to make our churches more bare than usual and to sing songs of exile and waiting. The tension between what goes on inside and outside our churches is most evident during these three or four weeks of December.

That tension exists on a deeper level as well. The consumerism and materialistic exploitation that characterize the "popular" celebration of the season are obvious and often lamented. Behind that consumerism is a message about the way things "ought to be." Spend money on this or your house will not look like the ones on the cards; nor will your family be the happy, harmonious, carol-singing fantasy seen on the TV specials. The only changes necessary are cosmetic and can be charged.

Americans, moreover, do not like to wait. In the land of fast food, the quick fix, and instant gratification, a voice crying out that Someone is coming but is not yet here will seldom seem like the herald of glad tidings.

As followers of Jesus, we need to be brought face to face with the tension that exists between our religious commitment and the values of our culture. Some segments of the American church, both Protestant and Catholic, conjure a myth of a Bible-believing, flag-waving America where God and country or religion and the good life are identified. But the questions our liturgical tradition of Advent poses are good questions. We have a need for challenge and for change. Unless we face the fact that we are not the picture-perfect people of the TV specials, "God's grace come as a Child" and returning in glory will have a difficult time calling us once again to wonder, to faith, to salvation.

What does this discussion have to do with the period of "devout and joyful expectation," which the Roman sacramentary describes ("General Norms for the Liturgical Year" 9)? Do we need another Lent? No, but I would submit that a genuine living of "expectation" leads a faithful Christian straight to repentance and a change of heart. We rejoice at the nearness of liberation and the dawning of the day of justice and become aware of the shadows that still lurk around us and within us. It is *God's* grace that we "devoutly" await. Nor is Lent all gloom as Lenten Preface I says: "Each year you give us this joyful season as we prepare to celebrate...with mind and heart renewed." There is joy during the journey as well as at the end.

Some portion of the "sacred three" of Lent (prayer and reflection on God's Word, charity, and fasting) are still needed in our personal lives if we as a community are to celebrate the season. There is the marvelous old German custom of having everyone in the family or the class draw names at the beginning of Advent, not for a Christmas gift exchange but as preparation. Every day, as secretly as possible, you must do at least one kindness for the person whose name you have drawn. Sometimes the crib is set up on the buffet, empty with a basket of straw alongside, so that each evening all who have carried out their promise of kindness can make the Child's bed a little softer.

Like any religious practice, this one can lend itself to superficiality or scrupulosity; but such simple, concrete, yet profound gestures are the true interconnection between liturgy and life.

Music and Color

What can be done to make our Sunday assemblies engaging celebrations of this season? First is the role of music. As with any other season, the melodies that keep running through our heads help us to carry the service forth. There is so much good music to sing besides "O Come, O Come, Emmanuel." The new edition of *Worship,* published by G.I.A. Publications, Inc., has some delightful metrical pieces. The many settings of Isaiah and of Psalms 25 and 80 are also appropriate. Using a common Gospel acclamation, response to the general intercessions, and Eucharistic acclamation can both tie the season together and set it apart.

Second is the role of the visual, especially of color. Some advocate the use of dark blue as more appropriate to the mood of the season than purple—a practice to which I have mixed reactions. On the one hand, if a rite as stylized as the Byzantine can survive without a fixed color cycle, so can the Roman. Moreover, I would like western Christians to explore a greater use of color. The Rite of Lyon has used gray during Lent for centuries—a very impressive alternative to the unremitting purple of the Roman Rite, especially for Ash Wednesday. Yellow can be as festive as white; blue and green could easily alternate during Ordinary Time, along with brown or tan for the autumn.

On the other hand, the reasons for dark blue in Advent seem shaky. Though the Mozarabic Rite and Sweden did make some use of this color for Advent, I have seen articles advocating the custom as a return to the Sarum Rite or to the Ambrosian—which it isn't. We have every right to start a new liturgical tradition; I am uncomfortable around people, though, who construct a fictitious past to justify it.

A linkage between Mary and blue has also been suggested. Yet Mary is not a major figure in the Advent Scripture readings. There is no mention of her on the first three Sundays. In the final eight days, she shares the focus with Joseph, Elizabeth, Zechariah, and throughout with John the Baptist. Though she is the pivotal figure in the final preparation for Christmas, the Advent lectionary and the nourishment it provides from the Word of God do not direct us toward Mary that often.

As some have pointed out, there are purples and purples. Vestments decorated with crowns of thorns and other instruments of the Passion are not appropriate for Advent just because they are purple. Some Episcopalians I know have suggested that we start distinguishing between Lenten purple, which is dark and dull and somber, and Advent purple, which is lighter and reddish and verging into that old rose shade (*not* pink!) that we have inherited for Gaudete and Laetare Sundays. Such a distinction seems worth developing.

The Wreath

The strongest visual element for Advent among American Christians is the Advent wreath. The difficulty is in successfully transferring the custom from home to church. The intimacy of lighting the small wreath on the dining room table simply cannot be recreated in church. The community's wreath must be big, capable of embracing many more hopes and yearnings. A twelve-inch wreath on a table on the side of the sanctuary with half-inch thick can--les is an invisible symbol; a three- or four- foot wreath suspended from the ceiling or mounted on a five-foot base or tripod is an immediately impressive sight.

The price we sometimes pay for such size is accessibility. If the wreath is suspended or if glass votive lights are used for the candles as a safety measure, there is no possibility of lighting the candles during the service (unless we are willing to accept the aluminum ladder as a liturgical object). Though the loss is unfortunate, a visible symbol without gesture seems better than an invisible symbol and an invisible gesture.

Integrating the wreath into the service is another challenge. The most obvious place for it, chosen by several communities of which I have been a member, is in the introductory rite as a call to worship. The accompanying "Blessing of the Wreath on Advent I" was originally composed by Rev. Joseph Lackner, S.M., and later re-edited and arranged.

The first version interjects a refrain just as in the General Intercessions; the second integrates the first three elements as tropes for the Kyrie. One of the presiders is asked to sing the Kyrie or Christe; a cantor could do so as well. Although an English "Lord have mercy" can be substituted, this is possibly a time for nostalgia and for teaching one of those simpler Gregorian chant melodies that many adults grew up with. Some further adaptation of this blessing can also be used on the second and third Sundays of Advent to link the first three Sundays even further.

A BLESSING
OF THE ADVENT WREATH (A)

While the Opening Hymn is being sung, the procession moves through the church, and everyone goes to the usual place. The following Blessing replaces the usual penitential rite or call to worship.

The Greeting

PC: In the name of the Father +, and of the Son, and of the Holy Spirit.

ALL: Amen.

PC: *(Greeting A, B, or C from the Order of Mass)*

ALL: And also with you.

The Invitation

The PC or an ACC gives an introductory call to worship, speaks of the meaning of the season and of the Sunday, and concludes with an invitation to silent prayer.

The Blessing

The refrain is played only once beforehand.

REFRAIN:

**Come, O Lord, and set us free.
Come, Lord Jesus, come! (Dameans)**

PC/ACC:
Circle of green,
    wreath of hopeful longing,
embracing times past and yet to come—
    faithful promise,
forever green,
    endless—
Lord, stir our hearts to hopeful yearning!

ALL: (Refrain)

Circle of purple,
    echoing the Baptist's call to turn our hearts
    from desperate ways—
Christ, change our hearts and help us live!

ALL: (Refrain)

Circle of white candle flame,
    melting wax of weeks and years gone by,
    but yet to come—
Lord, mark the time and light our way!

ALL: (Refrain)

Circle of hope be blessed +;
    make ready our hearts
for the Christmas guest.

ALL: Amen!

The Opening Prayer

A BLESSING
OF THE ADVENT WREATH (B)

While the Opening Hymn is being sung, the procession moves through the church, and everyone goes to the usual place. The following Blessing replaces the usual penitential rite or call to worship.

The Greeting

PC: In the name of the Father +, and of the Son, and of the Holy Spirit.

ALL: Amen.

PC: *(Greeting A, B, or C from the Order of Mass)*

All: And also with you.

The Invitation
The PC or an ACC gives an introductory call to worship, speaks of the meaning of the season and of the Sunday, and concludes with an invitation to silent prayer.

The Blessing
One of the CCs or the cantor may say or sing the invocation.

PC/ACC:
  Circle of green,
    wreath of hopeful longing,

29

embracing times past and yet to come—
    faithful promise, forever green, endless—
Lord, stir our hearts to hopeful yearning!
    Kyrie, eleison!

ALL: Kyrie, eleison!

PC/ACC:
 Circle of purple,
    echoing the Baptist's call to turn our hearts
    from desperate ways—
 Christ, change our hearts and help us live!
    Christe, eleison!

ALL: Christe, eleison!

PC/ACC:
 Circle of white candle flame,
    melting wax of weeks and years gone by,
    but yet to come—
 Lord, mark the time and light our way!
    Kyrie, eleison!

ALL: Kyrie, eleison!

PC/ACC:
 Circle of hope be blessed +;
    make ready our hearts
 for the Christmas guest.

ALL: Amen.

The Opening Prayer

The "O" Antiphons

The Fourth Sunday in Advent differs noticeably from the first three since it is focused both upon the events preparatory to the birth of the Messiah and upon the humble faith of Mary and Joseph and Elizabeth. The sense of anticipation that fills this Sunday's Scripture needs visual and musical expression.

An elaborate opening procession can be very effective. Over ten years ago, a parishioner made a series of large but portable banners based on the "O" antiphon titles as they occur in the hymn "O Come, O Come, Emmanuel." Banner carriers and ministers gather in the foyer. The leader of song announces the opening hymn beginning at the second stanza. While the organist plays an extended introduction, the banner carriers begin to move up the main aisle in single file, keeping quite far apart and holding the banners so that the images can be most readily seen.

As the first banner, "O Wisdom," enters the sanctuary, the community begins singing that stanza. If the spacing is accurate, each succeeding banner and verse are (relatively) synchronized—concluding with the "O Emmanuel" banner and stanza and the arrival of the ministers.

The banners are arranged in stands spread across the whole sanctuary, filling the space with color. The presider begins the Eucharist. The penitential rite is very brief, and the service is well begun.

Though the banners are not carried out at the end, the recessional can also be enhanced. My parish customarily sings "Long Ago Prophets Knew" (Oxford University Press) by F. Pratt Green to conclude this service. During the refrain, "Ring, bells, ring; sing, choirs, sing! When He comes, when He comes, who will make him welcome?", everyone rings bells they have brought from home. This is a simple, joyful anticipation of the Christmas feast.

READINGS AND PSALMS
FOR THE "O" ANTIPHONS

Parishes and schools, families and individuals often have some form of special prayer in preparation for Christmas. These devotions often involve the "O" Antiphons. Familiar from the hymn, "O Come, O Come Emmanuel," these refrains were originally the antiphons for the Canticle of Mary during the week before Christmas. Yet for many who use them in prayer, they can prove difficult to comprehend because of their rich use of biblical imagery.

The following readings and responsorial psalms are intended to be used during such devotions. Each passage either is one of the sources of that particular antiphon or has parallel imagery or theme.

December 17: O Wisdom

Wisdom 7:25-8:1
Psalm 104:1-2, 3-4, 5-6, 27-28, 29-30

REFRAIN: "Lord God, how great you are!"

Bless the Lord, my soul!
  Lord God, how great you are,
clothed in majesty and glory,
  wrapped in light as in a robe!

You stretch your heavens like a tent.
  Above the rains you build your dwelling.
You make the clouds your chariot;
  you walk on the wings of the wind.

You founded the earth on its base,
  to stand firm from age to age.
You wrapped it with the ocean like a cloak;
  the waters stood higher than the mountains.

All creatures look to you
  to give them their food in due season.
You give it, they gather it up;
  you open your hand, they have their fill.

You hide your face, they are dismayed;
  you take back your spirit, they die.
You send forth your spirit, they are created;
  and you renew the face of the earth.

December 18: O Sacred Lord of Israel (O Adonai)

Exodus 3:1-8, 13-15
Psalm 78:3-4, 4-5, 5-6, 7, 8

REFRAIN: "How glorious and mighty is the Lord!"

The things we have heard and understood,
  the things our forebears have told us—
these we will not hide from their children
  but tell them to the next generation:

the glories of the Lord and his might
  and the marvellous deeds he has done,
the witness he gave to Jacob,
  the law he established in Israel.

He gave a command to our forebears
   to make it known to their children
that the next generation might know it,
   the ones yet to be born.

They too should arise and tell their children
   that they too should set their hope in God
and never forget God's deeds
   but keep every one of his commands,

so that they might not be like their forebears,
   a defiant and rebellious race,
a race whose heart was fickle,
   whose spirit was unfaithful to God.

December 19: O Flower of Jesse's Stem

Isaiah 11:10-13, 15-16
Psalm 126:1-2, 2-3, 4-5, 6

**REFRAIN: "What marvels the Lord has
worked for us!"**

When the Lord delivered Zion from bondage,
   it seemed like a dream.
Then was our mouth filled with laughter,
   on our lips there were songs.

The heathens themselves said: What marvels
   the Lord worked for them!
What marvels the Lord worked for us!
   Indeed we were glad.

Deliver us, O Lord, from our bondage
    as streams in dry land.
Those who go sowing in tears
    will sing when they reap.

They go out, they go out, full of tears,
    carrying seed for the sowing;
they come back, they come back, full of song,
    carrying their sheaves.

December 20: O Key of David

Revelation 3:7-8, 10-13
Psalm 125:1, 2, 3, 4-5

**REFRAIN: "The Lord gives his people
   peace."**

Those who put their trust in the Lord
    are like Mount Zion, that cannot be shaken,
that stands forever.

Jerusalem! The mountains surround her,
    so the Lord surrounds his people
both now and forever.

For the scepter of the wicked shall not rest
    over the land of the just
for fear that the hands of the just
    should turn to evil.

Do good, Lord, to those who are good,
 to the upright of heart;
but the crooked and those who do evil,
 drive them away! On Israel, peace!

December 21: O Radiant Dawn

Isaiah 42:5-9
Psalm 107:10-11, 13-14, 15-16, 42-43

**REFRAIN: "The Lord's love endures
 forever!"**

Some lay in darkness and gloom,
 prisoners in misery and chains,
having defied the words of God
 and spurned the counsels of the Most High.

They they cried to the Lord in their need,
 and he rescued them from their distress.
He led them forth from darkness and gloom
 and broke their chains to pieces.

Let them thank the Lord for his kindness,
 for the wonders he does for his people:
for he bursts the gates of bronze
 and shatters the iron bars.

The upright see it and rejoice,
 but all who do wrong are silenced.
Let those who are wise observe these things.
 Let them ponder the love of the Lord.

December 22: O King of All Nations

Haggai 2:1-9
Psalm 92:5-6, 8-9, 13-14, 15-16

REFRAIN: "At the work of your hands I shout for joy!"

Your deeds, O Lord, have made me glad;
   for the work of your hands I shout with joy.
O Lord, how great are your works!
   How deep are your designs!

Though the wicked spring up like grass,
   and all who do evil thrive,
they are doomed to be eternally destroyed;
   but you, Lord, are eternally on high.

The just shall flourish like the palm-tree
   and grow like the Lebanon cedar.
Planted in the house of the Lord,
   they will flourish in the courts of our God,

still bearing fruit when they are old,
   still full of sap, still green,
to proclaim that the Lord is just.
   In him, my rock, there is no wrong.

December 23: O Emmanuel

Zechariah 2:10-17
Psalm 85:9-10, 11-12, 13-14

**REFRAIN: "His glory will dwell in our
land!"**

I will hear what the Lord God has to say,
    a voice that speaks of peace:
peace for his people and his friends
    and those who turn to him in their hearts.
His help is near for those who fear him,
    and his glory will dwell in our land.

Mercy and faithfulness have met;
    justice and peace have embraced.
Faithfulness shall spring up from the earth,
    and justice look down from heaven.

The Lord will make us prosper,
    and our earth shall yield its fruit.
Justice shall march before him,
    and peace shall follow his steps.

Other Ideas

Some parishes have the lovely tradition of a candlelight service of lessons and carols. The Episcopalian *Book of Occasional Services* has two versions: one for Advent and another for Christmastime. The structure of the service as usually celebrated, though, is not very sound liturgically.

The opening bidding prayer is very long and contains both introductory and intercessory material. The latter could easily be divided with the introductory material leading into a brief opening prayer. The intercessions could be reworked into a concluding general intercession leading into the Lord's Prayer, a final collect, and the appropriate seasonal solemn blessing. Such rearranging provides a more coherent movement within the service and involves the congregation in a significant way.

Another possibility would be to use the structure of sung Evening Prayer with the lessons and carols substituting for the psalmody and readings. Whatever the format, though, the planners must take care that the congregation is not given the role of spectator.

The scripture for Eucharist on the second and third Sundays of Advent makes those services particularly suitable for celebrating admission to the cate-chumenate or for welcoming those already baptized. (How to adapt the catechumenal rites to the Advent-Christmas season as a preparation for adult Baptism and/or profession of faith on the Baptism of the Lord is discussed in the chapter on the Rites Adapted for the Winter Cycle.)

Christmas

Sitting with my favorite aunt at Christmas Midnight Mass about twenty years ago, I was dozing a bit during the homily. The aging pastor had a gift for old-fashioned, pulpit-thumping oratory, but on great feasts his insecurity often led him to read at us from a book of sermons. One remark did get through to me, though, and produced an immediate response. When he declared, "Christmas is a feast of a Child for children," I leaned over and whispered to my aunt, "Then you end up with a childish religion."

The intervening years of participating in liturgy and of trying to live a Christian life have confirmed for me the truth of that spontaneous observation. The work of various Scripture scholars, especially Raymond Brown, has called believers to take a fresh look at the Christmas stories. More than just sentimental myths or children's fairy tales, they are part of the history of our redemption, intimately bound in with the dynamic of sin and forgiveness, of death and resurrection.

What we are called to celebrate is not that babies are cute and that the simple life is attractive (at least when you are not the one sleeping in the stable).

Instead we are called to glory anew in our humanity as the high point of God's creation. Despite our history of faithlessness, God did not give up on us. In the utterly human event of a baby's birth, faith sees a sacrament of God's faithfulness: promise, hope, a chance to begin again.

From my experience I would suggest that in planning an authentic celebration of Christmas, we need to consider several factors.

First, many people who attend have little faith commitment and are to some degree alienated from the Church. Yet the only proper response to their presence should be thankfulness for God's grace still at work, gracious hospitality, and an attempt to include them in the festivity.

Second, liturgy is *always* the work of the people. The great feasts especially should not be choir concerts or occasions for the pastor's fulsome rhetoric. All that is done to make the services "special" must be judged by a simple criterion: Will this element enhance or substitute for the community's participation? A choral anthem during the Presentation to which everyone can relax and listen can be an excellent prelude to the Eucharistic Prayer. A choral Gloria that leaves everyone standing for seven minutes can kill a service at its beginning.

Third, remembering the past is crucial to celebrating in the present. There is a need for continuity and even for nostalgia as well as for change and creativity. If everyone, even those who seldom come, are to be drawn into the service, the place, the actions, the music must feel in some sense like "home."

Fortunately our rich heritage of carols can provide a common ground on which to build Christmas services. Though capable of being bastardized, as in the medley of the first stanzas of five carols that I heard a choir do once, they often have—if sung in their entirety—some good theology and attractive images:

> I wonder as I wander out under the sky
> How Jesus the Savior did come for to die.
> (An Appalachian Carol)

Their evocative familiarity will entice into singing those who otherwise will attempt nothing more elaborate than "Happy Birthday."

Midnight Mass

The following is a common pattern for Midnight Mass celebrations:

1) musical prelude: with or without congregational participation;
2) special element: blessing the crib, placing the Infant in the manger, or proclaiming the Martyrology;
3) the Eucharist.

The problem with the first element, the musical prelude, is that it can easily become a mere concert or a timefiller until the real action starts. Yet to go all the way to a Christmas Vigil analogous to Easter Vigil means asking everyone to commit themselves to quite a long service during a time of many conflicting responsibilities. The structure of reading, musical response, meditative silence, and collective presidential prayer is a powerful tool for communal prayer, but not when people are wandering in during a thirty- to forty-minute period.

The following service of lessons and carols is an attempt to pull many factors together. Led by at least two readers and the musicians, it feels "looser" because there is no one "presiding." It is structured more or less historically, but one can walk in and pick up the story at any point. Highly musical, it makes some attempt to match up each reading and the subsequent carol. Silence would occur, for instance, only between each reading/carol unit. Yet the readings are proclaimed without the usual dialogue between reader and community. Done in semidarkness, the rite leads up to an extinguishing of all electric lights during the spoken Acclamations with their sung refrain—so that the Martyrology can be proclaimed by candlelight and the whole building flooded with light after the Introductory Rite.

CHRISTMAS MIDNIGHT MASS: LESSONS AND CAROLS

This portion of the service is led by the musicians and two or more readers. The ministers of the Mass may join in the service until the beginning of the reading from Theodotus, when they must retire to prepare.

The church is in semi-darkness, lit only enough to allow the community to sing the carols. The lectern is lit by two large candles standing on either side. Small hand-candles and collars are distributed to the community as they enter.

The service is timed to last for about thirty minutes. The readers take their places in the sanc-tuary just before the instrumental prelude.

The readers do not add "This is the Word of the Lord!" to the readings.

Prelude

Instruction

READER:
Dear People of God, during the season of Advent,
it has been our responsibility and joy
to prepare ourselves,
to hear once more the message of the angels,
to go to Bethlehem
and see the promised Savior
lying in a manger.

45

Let us hear in Holy Scripture
the story of God's loving purpose
from the time of our first parents' rebellion
until the glorious redemption brought to us
by his Holy Child, Jesus.
Let us begin our yearly celebration of Christ's birth
with our songs and hymns of praise.

Carol: "It Came Upon a Midnight Clear"

Lesson: from the Book of Genesis (3:12-15)

Adam replied, "It was the woman you put with me: she gave me the fruit and I ate it." Then the Lord God asked the woman, "What is this you have done?" The woman replied, "The serpent tempted me and I ate."

Then the Lord God said to the serpent, "Because you have done this, be accursed beyond all cattle and all wild beasts. I will make you enemies of each other: you and the woman, your offspring and her offspring. He will crush your head, and you will strike at his heel."

Carol: "O Little Town of Bethlehem"

Lesson: from the Book of Psalms (89:1-2, 3-4, 20, 26)

And King David said:
  "I will sing forever of your love, O Lord;
through all ages my mouth will proclaim your
    truth.
Of this I am sure: that your love lasts forever,
    that your truth is firmly established in
    heaven."

And God replied:
  "With my chosen one I have made a covenant;
I have sworn to David my servant:
  I will establish your dynasty forever
and set up your throne through all ages.

My hand shall always be with him;
    my arm shall make him strong.
He will say to me, 'You are my father,
    my God, the Rock who saves me!' "

Carol: "Away in a Manger" or "Once in Royal David's City"
(omitting the stanza "And through all his wondrous childhood")

Lesson: from the Book of Psalms (80:1-7, 14, 18-19)

From their exile in Babylon, the Israelites
    prayed:
"O Shepherd of Israel, hear us,
you who lead Joseph's flock;
    shine forth from your cherubim throne
upon Ephraim, Benjamin, Manasseh.
    O Lord, stir up your might;
    O Lord, come to our help.
God of hosts, bring us back;
    let your face shine on us, and we shall be
    saved!

Lord God of hosts, how long
    will you frown on your people's plea?
You have fed them with tears for their bread,
    and abundance of tears for their drink.
You have made us the taunt of our neighbors,
    our enemies laugh us to scorn.
God of hosts, bring us back;
    let your face shine on us, and we shall be
    saved!

God of hosts, turn again, we implore you;
    look down from heaven and see.
We will never forsake you again;
    give us life that we may call upon your name.
God of hosts, bring us back;
    let your face shine on us and we shall be
    saved!"

Carol: "Good Christian Friends, Rejoice"

Lesson: from "A Christmas Sermon" by Theodotus, Bishop of Ancyra

The Lord of all comes in the form of a servant; and he comes as a poor human being, so that he will not frighten away those he seeks to capture like a hunter. He is born in an obscure town, deliberately choosing a humble dwelling-place. His mother is a simple maiden, not a great lady. And the reason for all this lowly state is so that he can gently ensnare humankind and bring us to salvation. If he had been born amid the splendor of a rich family, unbelievers would surely have said that the face of the world had been changed by the power of wealth. If he had chosen to be born in Rome, the greatest of cities, they would have ascribed the same change to the power of her citizens.

Suppose our Lord had been the son of an emperor: they would have pointed to the advantage of authority. Imagine his father a legislator; their cry would have been, "See what can be brought about by the law." But, in fact, what did he do? He chose nothing but poverty and mean surroundings, everything that was plain and ordinary and, in the eyes of most people, obscure. And this so that it could be clearly seen that the Godhead alone transformed the world. That was why he chose his mother from among the poor of a very poor country, and became poor himself.

This is the lesson of the crib.

(*Hom la in die Nativitatis Domini,* 77, 1360-1; translated in *A Word in Season*, ed. Henry Ashworth, O.S.B., Dublin: The Talbot Press, 1973, 71-2 rev.)

Carol: "See Amid the Winter's Snow" or "On This Day"

Lesson: from the Book of Isaiah the Prophet (7:10-14)

Once again the Lord spoke to King Ahaz and said, "Ask the Lord your God for a sign for yourself coming either from the depths of hell or from the heights above." "No," Ahaz answered, "I will not put the Lord to the test."

Then he said, "Listen now, House of David: are you not satisfied with trying the patience of mortals without trying the patience of my God too? The Lord himself therefore will give you a sign. It is this: the maiden is with child and will soon give birth to a son whom she will call Emmanuel."

ADVENT PROCESSION

Donald Pearson

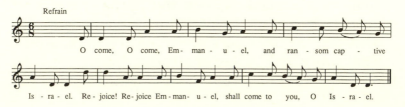

© 1987 Donald Pearson

Acclamations

REFRAIN:

O come, O come, Emmanuel, and ransom captive Israel.

Rejoice! Rejoice! Emmanuel shall come to you, O Israel.

A: Jesus is the long-awaited Messiah,
our promised Redeemer.

B: Jesus is the Savior—the name revealed to Joseph the just by the angel.

(Refrain)

A: Jesus is the Son of the Most High;
Gabriel announced his coming to the Virgin Mary.

B: Jesus is the Holy One of God;
in his presence John the Baptist leapt for joy in Elizabeth's womb.

(Refrain)

A: Jesus is the Rising Sun;
Zechariah foretold that he would shine on all who sit in darkness and in the shadow of death.

B: Jesus is the Light and the Glory of his people;
for him Simeon and Anna and all the just waited and longed.

(Refrain)

A: Jesus is Emmanuel,

B: God-with-us!

(Refrain)

The readers immediately go to sit in the places they will occupy during the Mass.

Four or more people now come up from the congregation, light their small candles from the candles by the lectern, and go out to light the small candles of those sitting at the end of the pews, so that the light can quickly spread throughout the church.

As soon as the lighting has begun, two readers (A and B) step up to the lectern, and the musicians begin the refrain for the Acclamations.

The Martyrology

This involves two readers (A and B) and bells.

One or two bearers of hand-chimes immediately lead the two readers from the back of the church up the main aisle. The readers carry small candles.

The bearers of the bells stop in the main aisle about ten feet from the sanctuary step; the readers move past them and up to the sanctuary, standing about eight feet apart.

The bells should ring softly during the procession and stop when the reading begins.

A: In the 5199th year after the creation of the world, from the time when in the beginning God created the heavens and the earth;

B: In the 2957th year after the flood;

52

A: In the 2015th year after the birth of Abraham;

B: In the 1510th year after the time of Moses and the going forth of the people of Israel from Egypt;

A: In the 1032nd year after the anointing of King David;
In the 65th week according to the prophecy of Daniel;

A and B: In the 194th Olympiad of the Greeks;

A: In the 752nd year after the foundation of the city of Rome;
In the 42nd year of the reign of Octavian Augustus;

B: While all the world was at peace;
The bells start softly. The readers begin crescendo.

A and B: Jesus the Messiah, Eternal God,

B: And Son of the Eternal Father,

A: Yearning in mercy to make the world holy by his coming,

B: Having been conceived by the Holy Spirit,

A: Nine months after his conception,

B: Was born in Bethlehem of Juda—

A and B: Born as one of us from the Virgin Mary!

The bells ring loudly and then stop.

A: December 25th: the Birthday of our Lord Jesus the Messiah, according to the flesh.

The Processional Song begins immediately. The readers turn, bow to the altar, and go to their places for the Mass. The ministers enter in procession, carrying small candles as does the rest of the community.
The Mass continues as usual; the candles are extinguished after the Opening Prayer.

The Midnight Mass Eucharist does not need much elaboration. Doing well what is given in the lectionary and sacramentary will produce a moving service. Attention to details, though, will keep all the different components in balance. Music must not be overwhelming and should blend the choral and the congregational. The General Intercessions must be carefully prepared. Given the variety of Christmas Prefaces, a thematic continuity can be established between the homily and the Eucharistic Prayer. Or would one of the other five approved Eucharistic Prayers be more appropriate? Automatically choosing the shortest is a false kindness. If people choose to come to a late night service, they deserve a little substance in return.

There are two points in the service where small adaptations can make a special impact (cf., page 16, "Christmas Midnight Mass: The Communion Rite"). First, since the Gospel ends with the song of the angels, the proclamation can conclude with the whole community joining in two stanzas of "Angels

We Have Heard On High" as an extended concluding dialogue. If there is a program, everyone may
sing the verses. If not, the gospeller or the cantor
sings the stanzas while everyone joins in the familiar refrain.

Gospel: Luke 2:1-14

*The organist softly begins the melody to "Angels
We Have Heard On High" at about verse ten and
leads the community into singing the following stanzas when the song of the angels is reached.*

Gloria in excelsis Deo! (twice)

Angels we have heard on high
Sweetly singing o'er the plains,
And the mountains in reply
Echoing their joyous strains:

"Gloria in excelsis Deo!" (twice)

Come to Bethlehem and see
Him whose birth the angels sing;
Come, adore on bended knee
Christ the Lord, the newborn King.

"Gloria in excelsis Deo!"

*After the Lord's Prayer, the usual Prayer for Peace
could be omitted, with the following carol taking its
place.*

The Exchange of Peace

ACC/PC: On the night of Jesus' birth, the angels sang: "Glory to God in the highest, and peace to his people on earth!" Let us pray that God's peace come to us and to the world and join together in song.

Now to the Lord sing praises,
All you within this place,
And with true love and fellowship
each other now embrace:
This holy tide of Christmas
Now brings to us its grace—
O tidings of comfort and joy,
Comfort and joy,
O tidings of comfort and joy!

PC: May the peace of the Lord be with you all!

ALL: And also with you!

ACC/PC: Let us now exchange peace with one another.

Christmas Day Mass

The question of the advisability of "vigil" Masses and conveniently scheduled "family" or "children's" Masses is under discussion among American Catholics. Whatever the outcome, the fact remains that there will continue to be people who celebrate Christmas on Christmas Day. To me, the unfortunate development is the rubric allowing the interchange of the lectionary selections among any of the Masses. The close ties between the time of day and the sacramentary are maintained while the more subtle yet genuine ties with the readings are destroyed. In practice, everyone hears Luke 2:1-14.

There is still a need during the Day Eucharist to proclaim the more concrete pictures of Luke's Gospel. Some of the best homilies I have heard have been on John's prologue, but the younger members of the community cannot easily "see" its images.

Having spent my adult life worshiping in Jesuit parishes, I am familiar with their tradition of the proclamation of the Martyrology before Midnight Mass. The custom of blessing the crib or of placing the Infant in the manger could therefore be adapted as the prelude to the Day Eucharist, especially since there are many more children in attendance.

The "station" at the crib given here is similar to the station that begins the Palm Sunday procession: greeting, gospel, instruction, blessing, procession (the gospel is omitted before a Dawn Eucharist). The blessing is based on a text by Linda C. Hall in *Living Worship,* October 1980. The invitation to the procession is based on the gospel just proclaimed. Since this service immediately precedes the Eucharist, omitting the Pentitential Rite is appropriate.

CHRISTMAS DAY EUCHARIST

While the community is gathering, all are encouraged to make a visit at the crib, especially if everyone will not be able to gather around it later.

When it is time for the service to begin, the readers, acolytes, concelebrants, and other ministers with candles and bells gather without formal procession at the crib. The PC then faces the community, greets them, and invites everyone to gather around the crib if that is possible. If the community is too large, all are invited to face the crib, and the children, at least, are invited to gather around if possible.

The Gathering

PC: In the name of the Father, and of the Son, + and of the Holy Spirit.

ALL: Amen!

PC (Greeting A, B, or C from the Order of Mass.)

ALL: And also with you.

PC/ACC: (*An invitation in his own words to gather at the crib.*)

When all have gathered, a reader proclaims the Gospel of the Dawn Mass.

The Gospel: Luke 2:15-20

The Instruction and Veneration

The PC/ACC speaks briefly about the meaning of the reading and the crib. At the end he invites all to join in some act of veneration. Possibly everyone can kneel for a few moments; the crib can be incensed.

The Blessing of the Crib

PC/ACC: Let us (stand and) pray.

We praise you; we thank you,
Father, mighty Lord;
To set us free, you sent your only Son
to be born in great humility of the Virgin Mary.
A lowly cave was his birth-place;
the animals' manger was his first cradle.
Yet all the while the angels sang of his glory
to those who kept watch,
yearning for news of salvation.

Bless now + this Christmas crib.
Let it reveal to us once again
the great love of our Savior,
and bring us with the shepherds and wise men
to give back to him in true devotion
all that we have—and even our very selves.

All praise and thanksgiving be yours, Father,
through Jesus your Son,
truly God and truly human,
living and reigning with you and the Holy Spirit,
now and forever and ever.

ALL: Amen.

The Procession

ACC/PC:
Treasuring all that we have seen and heard here
and pondering it within our hearts,
let us glorify and praise God together
as we go now to his altar.

The prelude to the Processional Hymn begins immediately, and those gathered around are informally sent back to their seats. When all have had an opportunity to return to their places, the first stanza of the Processional Hymn is begun. The procession of the ministers moves from the crib, through the church, and to the usual place in the sanctuary.

Processional Hymn: "O Come, All Ye Faithful"

The Pentitential Rite, Kyrie, and Gloria are omitted. The ministers reverence the altar and go to their places. When the Hymn is finished, the PC proclaims the Opening Prayer.

Further adaptations of this rite, especially for children, are easy. Rather than a separate family or children's celebration, involving the children in proclaiming the Gospel or in placing the various figures in the scene would be significant but simple ways for them to participate. Venerating the crib with incense, for example, can be impressive, as long as sparks and straw stay separate.

A final observation: many of the texts from the lectionary and sacramentary and hymnal speak of Baptism in relation to the Incarnation:

Born to raise those sprung from earth,
Born to give us second birth.
("Hark, the Herald Angels Sing")

Yet I feel that Christmas is not the most appropriate feast in the winter cycle for the *public* celebration of Infant Baptism. Sometimes because families have gathered from far away, Baptisms must be celebrated. The Baptism of the Lord, which concludes the winter cycle, is *the* time for involving the whole community in such services. Appropriate adaptations are presented in the chapter on that feast.

Rites of
Adult Initiation

In this chapter, "old RCIA" refers to the "Rite of Christian Initiation of Adults" in Rites of the Catholic Church I (New York: Pueblo Publishing Co., 1976). "New RCIA" refers to Rite of Christian Initiation of Adults (Study Edition) (Chicago: Liturgy Training Publications, 1988).

The rites of Christian initiation as currently structured remain true to the vision of Christian antiquity in arranging the chronology of all the rites around the Easter Vigil. The readings, prayers, and rituals of almost fourteen weeks of the year are thus focused either upon preparing the community and the elect for the celebration of initiation or upon unfolding the meaning of that celebration. No one who has experienced this liturgical ensemble can ever doubt its potential for power and grace in the lives of all involved.

Yet, as Christian antiquity knew, not everyone fits into the standard time frame. The Epiphany (or Theophany, the Byzantine tradition's name) as another major occasion for the communal celebration of initiation goes back to the very roots of the feast. Even the development of Advent in its various forms seems to have been much influenced by a desire to create some sort of preparatory period for Epiphany Baptisms analogous to Lent (cf., e.g., Adolf Adam, *The Liturgical Year.*) Thus the possibility of using the winter cycle for those catechumens or candidates who do not fit into the Easter chronology is not suggesting something foreign to the history or the theology of that portion of the church year. Indeed, the Episcopal Church in the latest *Book of Occasional Services* has not only provided texts for a Baptismal Vigil for the Feast of the Baptism of the Lord but has also suggested the use of their version of the Rite of Election on Advent I with Scrutinies on Advent II, III, and IV. That suggested format can alert us, though, to the potential danger of "initiation overkill" if we make too frequent use of the winter cycle for the full rites of initiation. To ask a Christian community to move through the final preparatory phase for initiation in December and early January and then to begin again in mid or late February is asking a great deal. Yet such rites present a better alternative to either "private" Baptism or to the omission of all preparatory rites, if they are celebrated with appropriate adaptations and a sensitivity to the community.

The following rites represent an attempt at such an adaptation. Though founded upon our customary rituals for Lent, various ceremonies have been changed in number, in sequence, and in wording. (A community involved in this cycle would also *not* celebrate admission to the catechumenate or welcoming the already baptized in preparation for Easter during this period. Interlocking the two cycles would be confusing for most parishioners.)

Election and Enrollment of Names is celebrated on Advent I. The major change is the text for the Presentation of the Catechumens and/or Candidates. Though a bit longer than the corresponding one for Lent, this seems the best moment to explain the theology behind this adaptation of the rites to the community.

Since the number being presented is presumably small, the witness of the godparents/sponsors has been changed from ritualized questions into *brief* personal statement. Experience has shown the power of such public testimony for Catholics who have never experienced such personal involvement within a formal structure. The entire assembly's approval of the catechumens/candidates (cf. RCIA, old 144, new 118) is also given verbal expression by a dialogue based on the admission to the catechumenate.

This series of affirmation is climaxed by the presider's declaration of Election, followed by the Enrollment as the gesture acting out that call. From a dramatic standpoint, this reversal of the rite's order is much more effective.

Aside from minor substitutions from "Lent" and "Easter" to more generic terms, only two other texts needed fuller adaptation: the presider's invitation to communal prayer and the dismissal of the elect. The latter has been changed into a blessing since that seems to be the usual way to exit the assembly, even for catechumens (cf. RCIA, old 119, new 95).

A RITE FOR ELECTION AND ENROLLMENT OF NAMES — ADVENT I

This rite may be used for the nonbaptized, the already baptized, or a group composed of both. It may be concelebrated. A deacon may also concelebrate it.

After the Homily the Creed is omitted. The presbyter who is to conduct the rite (and the concelebrants) comes to the head of the main aisle while the community remains seated. The chief catechist goes to the lectern.

The parish register and a suitable pen are prepared in advance on the altar, with separate pages for the baptized and nonbaptized to sign, or else only the nonbaptized are asked to sign.

The Presentation of the Catechumens and Candidates and Their Election

PC/ACC: (*addressing the community in these or similar words*)
Brothers and sisters,
as Advent begins, we recall once again
that God's Son once lived among us.
He was as human as we are:
born as a child, sharing our sorrow and joy,
our weakness and our hope.
He was as human as we are;
yet he came to change us,
to fulfill our hope
and set us free from our weakness.

By Baptism he has given us new birth,
a rebirth as God's own sons and daughters.

And so as we keep watch
for the Lord Jesus to come again in glory,
it is our privilege and responsibility today
to call others to a new share in our common life,
and to help them prepare
for the sacraments of initiation
on the feast of the Lord Jesus's Baptism.
We who know them
consider them to be sincere in their desire
and wish you all to ratify our decision today.

CATECHIST: (*addressing the catechumens and candidates*) Catechumens and candidates, as I call your names, would you please stand and come forward with your sponsors.

As their names are called, the candidates come forward and stand on the step of the sanctuary, facing the congregation.

One of his/her sponsors goes to the lectern and speaks briefly about that person's preparation. The sponsors then stand behind the catechumen or candidate, facing the congregation.

When all have been presented, the PC/ACC comes down to the center of the main aisle and faces the catechumens and candidates.

PC/ACC: (*addressing the catechumens and candidates*) Having heard the witness of your catechist and sponsors, you must now express your own intention clearly before the whole Church assembled here.

(*Addressing the Catechumens*)
N (&N),
do you wish to share in Christ's sacraments
of entry into his Church:
in baptism, confirmation, and the eucharist?

CATECHUMENS: Yes, I do!

PC/ACC (*addressing the already baptized*):
N (&N),
do you wish to enter into full communion
by making your profession of faith and by sharing
(in confirmation and) in the eucharist?

CANDIDATE(S): Yes, I do!

PC/ACC: (*addressing the congregation*)
Brothers and sisters,
though these catechumens and candidates
may not be known to you personally,
it is still our common task to give them
the example of Christian life,
our communal responsibility
to lead them to the sacraments.

And so, if you are willing to help in this task,
I ask you to respond: Yes, I am ready!
to the following questions.

With Christ as your witness and help, are all of you ready to help N&N/these catechumens and candidates to know and follow Christ more fully?

ALL: Yes, I am ready!

PC/ACC: Are you ready to continue your support of these catechumens and candidates by the witness of your Christian lives?

ALL: Yes, I am ready!

PC/ACC: Are you ready to continue your support in your prayers and your fellowship?

ALL: Yes, I am ready!

PC/ACC: (*turning to address the catechumens and candidates*)
N&N/Catechumens and candidates,
in the name of this community
and of the whole Church,
and in the name of Christ
who is present among us,
I call you now to the sacraments of initiation!

The PC/ACC leads the community in applause.

(*Addressing the elect*)
In token of this call,
come and enroll your name in our parish register.

The PC (and concelebrants) steps up behind the altar. With the help of the catechists, the elect also come up behind, facing the congregation, to sign their names. They then return to the front of the sanctuary, but now stand with their sponsors behind them with everyone facing the altar.

The community meanwhile is seated and sings a brief song or refrain.

When everyone has returned to his/her place, the PC/ACC stands again at the head of the main aisle, facing the elect and the congregation, and introduces the General Intercessions.

The Prayer for the Elect

PC/ACC: (*addressing the elect*)

Elect, it is your duty now to ask the help of our Father. Remember that he is ever faithful to those whom he has called to himself.

(*Addressing the sponsors*)

Sponsors, these elect have been entrusted to you in the Lord. In sign of the support you will continue to give them, please place your hand on their shoulders.

(*Addressing the community*)

Brothers and sisters,
let us now pray for N&N/these elect
and for ourselves
that we might be strengthened
in the coming weeks
by our mutual efforts,
and come together
to the glory that Jesus has promised.

An acolyte or reader proclaims various petitions for the elect and for other intentions according to the usual pattern for the General Intercessions. A presbyter concludes with a prayer.

PRESBYTER:
Father, God of power and love,
you wish to make everything new in Christ
and to call all people to full life in him.
Guide and direct N&N/these elect.
Keep them faithful to the call they have received.
Build them into the living Body of your Son,
and prepare them to be sealed
with the promised gift of the Holy Spirit.
This we ask through Christ
who is Lord forever and ever.

ALL: Amen!

The Blessing and Dismissal of the Elect

ACC/PC: (*addressing the elect*) Elect, bow your heads and pray for God's blessing!

The presider pauses for a moment, then continues:

You have been chosen by God
and have entered with us on the journey of faith;
and so may the blessing of almighty God:
the Father +, the Son, and the Holy Spirit,
come down upon you and remain with you forever.

ALL: Amen!

ACC/PC: Go in peace until we meet again.

The elect then leave for further instruction. The Eucharist continues with the Presentation of the Gifts by the sponsors.

A scrutiny could be celebrated on Advent III. The season of Advent and especially the two Sundays that portray John the Baptist deal already with the call to repentance that is at the heart of this service. (In Cycle C the fuller readings from the Common Lectionary would be more forceful: Philippians 4:4-9 and Luke 3:7-18.) Though another scrutiny could be held on Advent II, one *is* the legal minimum (cf. RCIA, old 52, new 20), and overkill is a real problem. The markedly different character of Advent IV makes it unsuitable for such a rite. (The new rite's insistence on using the readings and texts from the Lenten A cycle whenever the scrutinies are celebrated [cf. RCIA, new 133] is a development that I am not pleased with. Not all of the scrutiny texts are that closely tied to the Johannine Gospels.)

The following proposals are based on the rite found in the 1974 provisional text edition of the RCIA. The only major textual adaptation is in the Invitation and Instruction. Again, because of the presumably small number, the concluding blessing incorporates a strong gesture: the presider's laying of hands upon each individual with an appropriate formula and communal response.

A RITE OF REPENTANCE AND SOLEMN BLESSING—ADVENT III

The Penitential Rite at the beginning of Eucharist is omitted.
Immediately after the Homily the Creed is omitted. The community remains seated; the presbyter (and concelebrating deacon or presbyter) who is to lead the rite comes to the head of the main aisle. The catechist prepares to guide the elect and their sponsors.

The Invitation and Instruction

CATECHIST: (*addressing the elect from the lectern*) Elect, as I call your names, would you please come forward with your sponsors.

When called, the elect come to stand across the front of the sanctuary with their sponsors behind them, all facing the altar.

PC/ACC: (*addressing the community*)
Brothers and sisters, as Advent continues,
we rejoice today that our God is very near to us.
Yet we also hear today
the voice of John the Baptist,
calling us to repentance, to a change of heart.
Our share in the life of the Spirit,
though real, is imperfect.
N & N/these elect have heard
that same call to holiness
and wish to share with us more fully in God's life.

73

And so let us pray for these elect;
let us pray for ourselves.
With repentance and faith in our hearts,
let us kneel and pray.

*The elect, sponsors, ACC, and PC kneel on the
sanctuary step. Everyone else kneels in his/her place.*

The General Intercessions

*A catechist, acolyte, or reader leads the petitions.
At the end a presbyter stands, faces the congregation, and concludes with a prayer.*

PRESBYTER:
God of power,
you created us in your image and likeness
and formed us in holiness and justice.
Even when we sinned against you,
you did not abandon us,
but in your wisdom chose to save us
by sending your Son as one of us.

Now free these elect from evil;
keep far from them the spirit of wickedness,
falsehood and greed.
Open their hearts to understand your Gospel.
As full members of your Church,
may they bear witness to your truth
and put into practice your commands of love.
This we ask through Christ
who is Lord forever and ever.

ALL: Amen!

The Blessing

The ACC and PC then stand and turn toward the elect.)

ACC/PC: Sponsors, please stand and place your hands on the shoulders of the elect.

(The PC then lays his hands on the heads of each of the elect. To each he says the following words.)

N, may Jesus free you from your sins
and fill you with his life.

ALL: (sing) Amen. Amen.

The nonbaptized can be anointed instead with the Oil of Catechumens.

Dismissal

When all the elect have been blessed or anointed, they are dismissed.

ACC/PC:
Go in peace now,
and may Christ be your strength
until we meet again.

The elect then leave for further instruction. The Eucharist continues as the sponsors make the Presentation of the Gifts.

Since the Presentation of the Profession of Faith is not penitential in character, it could be celebrated on the Epiphany. The feast's proclamation of God's revelation in Jesus works well with the rite. Again a few generic textual changes are necessary, but the major revisions are in the Invitation and Presentation and in the concluding Blessing. Ritually, the Ephphetha could also be added at the end of the Creed to act out the entrusting of the Catholic faith to the elect.

A RITE FOR
THE PRESENTATION OF
THE PROFESSION OF
FAITH—EPIPHANY

The Penitential Rite at the beginning of the Eucharist is omitted.

This rite may be used for the nonbaptized or the baptized, depending on their prior religious formation, or a group composed of both (cf., National Statutes for the Catechumenates #31). Its purpose is to prepare both the elect and the community for Baptismal Vows.

This rite may be concelebrated. A deacon may also lead or concelebrate it.

After the Homily the presbyter (and concelebrants) who is to lead the rite comes to the head of the main aisle. The chief catechist goes to the lectern. The community remains seated.

The Invitation and Presentation

CATECHIST: (*addressing the community in these or similar words*)
Brothers and sisters,
five weeks ago we assumed
a common responsibility
to lead N & N/these elect
to the sacraments of initiation
at the feast of the Baptism of the Lord Jesus.
Even though we may not be personally involved
in their preparation, each one of us is still called
to give them the witness of our Christian lives,

and to support them
with our prayers and fellowship.

Today as we celebrate the Epiphany,
we proclaim that in Jesus
the light of faith has dawned
not only for Israel but for all human history.
And so it is fitting that we share today
in the final preparation of these elect
by officially handing over to them
within this community
that Creed which is the basis of our common faith
and of our common life in God.

(*Addressing the elect*)
Elect, as I call your name, please come forward
with your sponsor.

*When called, the elect come forward and line up
across the front, facing the altar with their sponsors
behind them.*

PC/ACC: (*addressing the elect from the head of the
main aisle*)
As your preparation
for the sacraments of initiation continues,
it is time for you to be entrusted by this community
with our Church's Profession of Faith.
By this faith everyone here
has been brought to share in God's own life,
through Christ and in the power of the Holy Spirit.
The words of our Profession are few;
the mysteries they express are awesome.

Listen to them, therefore,
with a sincere and open heart;
reflect upon them and pray over them.
Soon you will share more fully in God's own life
by professing them together with us.

(*Addressing the community*)
And so, brothers and sisters, let us stand now and
make our common profession of faith.

*The PC/ACC leads the community in the Nicene
Creed.*

The Ephphetha

PC/ACC: Sponsors, I invite you now to mark the
elect with the sign of faith; and I invite this whole
community to repeat these words after me.

*PC/ACC should pause momentarily at the
asterisks in the text.*

(*On the ears*)
Christ opened the ears of the deaf.*
In his name we say to you:*
Ephphetha, be opened!* +
May you hear his call to faith.*

(*On the mouth*)
Christ opened the mouth of the dumb*
and gave them speech.*
In his name we say to you:*
Ephphetha, be opened!* +

May you profess the faith you have heard*
to the glory and praise of God.*

General Intercessions

The General Intercessions follow immediately, beginning with special intentions for the elect. A presbyter concludes with a prayer.

PRESBYTER:
All-powerful Father, ever-living God,
fountain of life and truth, source of eternal love,
hear our prayers for N & N/these elect.
Make them holy by a new gift of your Spirit.
Give them true knowledge, firm hope,
and sound teaching.
May they be ready to profess
and to live their baptismal faith.
This we ask through Christ
who is Lord forever and ever.

ALL: Amen!

Blessing and Dismissal of the Elect

ACC/PC: (*addressing the elect*) Elect, bow your
heads and pray for God's blessing!

The presider pauses for a moment, then continues:

PC:
As God once guided the Magi,
so may he guide you on your journey of faith;

and may the blessing of almighty God:
the Father +, the Son, and the Holy Spirit,
come down upon you and remain with you forever.

ALL: Amen!

ACC/PC: Go in peace till we meet again.

*The elect then leave for further instruction. The
Eucharist continues as the sponsors make the Presentation of Gifts.*

The Preparation Rites of Holy Saturday can be used unaltered at a semi-public service during the week before the Baptism of the Lord.

The actual rites of adult initiation on the Baptism of the Lord would be the same as at Easter Vigil. Some of the same textual alterations for the celebration of Infant Baptism suggested in the chapter on that feast are also suitable and are outlined there.

The cycle presented here is only an initial adaptation. How to celebrate RCIA, whether centered around Easter or some other festival, is undergoing rapid evolution in this country. My greatest fear is that we will be locked too quickly into one pattern before we have had the chance to hear from the grassroots about the concrete realities of trying to make this model of Christian formation come alive for the first time in over a millennium.

The Baptism of the Lord

Many of the ideas treated here were also explored in "Promises Remembered: A Rite of Renewal," Liturgy 4, no. 3 (Summer 1984).

Those familiar with the Byzantine and other Eastern Christian traditions as they are being lived even today in America become aware of how much the great liturgical families share in common. The great festivals of Easter, Pentecost, and Christmas provide the foci around which communal worship, art, and piety have shaped the prayer and the lives of countless believers.

The one outstanding divergence among the shared ancient feasts is the significance of the January 6 celebration. In the Roman tradition, the Epiphany proclaims the revelation of the newborn King of the Jews to the Gentile Magi. In the Byzantine and other Eastern traditions, the Theophany celebrates the Baptism of Jesus in the Jordan. Rather than dwelling upon gold, frankincense, and myrrh, the liturgy includes a great blessing of water—not only in church but at a nearby lake or stream. Not the birth of the Savior but the rebirth of those saved by Baptism dominates the imagery of the hymns and prayers. The myths of the infancy narratives yield to the historical events that define the public life and ministry of Jesus.

Only with the reform of the Roman lectionary and calendar around 1970 did this event and celebration enter into the ongoing awareness of Catholic Sunday assemblies as the inauguration (in most years) of Ordinary Time. We have thus only begun to explore in our personal and communal prayer life the significance of this portion of the Gospel. Why might this event be both essential and challenging (not to say disturbing) to our identity as Christians? I would submit that the answer is fourfold.

First, the Baptism of Jesus is paradigmatic. If a parish community regularly celebrates Infant Baptism as a public rite within Sunday Eucharist and full adult initiation annually at Easter Vigil, and if we become that "conversion community" that the bishops call us to be in their approval of the adapted RCIA (cf. RCIA, new 9), then we are going to have to explore again what we mean by Baptism. No longer will we be content with references to "washing away original sin" as we experience both in worship and in shared life what Christian initiation is all about, and that quest will lead us not only to Jesus's death and resurrection but to *his* Baptism.

This exploration has already begun in the varied scriptural accounts that the early Church has entrusted to us. The event is being understood already as reminiscent of the Genesis 1 creation account in which the Spirit hovered over the waters from which life was to arise. It is also reminiscent of the exodus event: Jesus embodies a new Israel. Having passed through the waters, he goes off to the desert for forty days to explore his relationship with God. Jesus is also seen in solidarity with all the others who have come seeking repentance and forgiveness; yet the Johannine account hails him as the "Lamb" who would "take away the sins of the world." Clearly these multiple interpretations indicate that the earliest Christian communities found something extremely significant in their recalling and retelling of this event from Jesus' life.

Second, the core of this significance is found, I think, in the *inward* reality of the event. In the gospels sometimes some of those present are aware that something is happening, but all of them portray Jesus as experiencing within himself both the presence and the call of God in a radically new way. All the interpretations that the various accounts propose are attempts to come to grips with the new identity and mission of this middle-aged Jew.

For catechumenate teams and charismatic prayer groups, for ordinary Christians who regularly celebrate Infant Baptism and adult initiation, and for those being initiated, this event's inward reality is somehow paradigmatic. The fire, wind, and tongue-speaking of Pentecost were public, dramatic, and ultimately transitory; an intense, transforming, and *personal* relationship with God is not.

Third, not only is the personal character of this relationship normal for Christians but also its confusion and puzzlement. The synoptics all link Jesus' Baptism with his fast and temptation in the desert. Only through prayer and meditation upon the Scriptures and trial-and-error does the synoptic Jesus discover what his identity and mission are. As John L. McKenzie says: "He is not the royal conquering messiah but the servant who proclaims and suffers" (*Jerome Biblical Commentary* 2, 43:24, 68) Jesus's struggle is the model for our struggle as we too strive to discover the implications of our Baptism for our values, our relationships, and our lives. And like Jesus we find that sometimes the truth of our Baptism is found in bitter suffering (Mark 10:38-40).

Fourth, the terms that define that new relationship with God are also *somehow* paradigmatic. The voice from heaven addresses Jesus as "my son." The gender of this title is not its significant component; the title is not primarily an anatomical statement. It is perhaps a conscious substitute for the "servant" of Isaiah 42:1 proclaiming the new intimacy between God and the chosen and beloved one, who will both struggle with and perfectly fulfill the divine will.

The correlative term "Father" has also been regarded in Christian tradition as somehow paradigmatic. Because one of the great spiritual questions of the contemporary age is inclusive language, we must struggle with this term in a new way. As we struggle, I would suggest that we follow the advice of the Letter to the Hebrews and "keep our eyes fixed on Jesus who leads us in our faith and brings it to perfection" (Hebrews 12:2, NJB).

Jesus is not a philosopher describing how mere mortals can speak meaningfully about the Holy Mystery. Nor is he a Jungian exploring the rich variety of his archetypal consciousness. Nor is he a child dealing with his experience through imaginative projection. He is a Jew who knows that God both transcends yet works within time and history. He is, himself, an individual who is portrayed as having just undergone a most profound encounter with his people's God. And the word that he is portrayed as using throughout his subsequent ministry to address again and again that God he encountered is "Father."

Like "son," the emphasis is not upon anatomy but upon relationship. Yet we must take the term seriously because Jesus took it seriously. Terms like "patriarchy" and "androcentric bias" are relevant to the discussion but should not be used too quickly. We must take the experience of Jesus as seriously as we take our own, for Christian life at its core is life *through* Jesus and *with* Jesus and *in* Jesus.

How are we to celebrate such a festival? How can we explore the riches of this feast? We should continue our celebration of Christmas. Like Pentecost, the Baptism of the Lord is an end that is also a beginning, but it should be clearly an ending. The green and red of Christmas and the gold of Epiphany can lead into the red and white of the Baptism. Most of the seasonal decorations should remain, but the manger scene can be removed and replaced by the baptismal font or the sprinkling bowl.

The seasonal acclamations and refrains should be maintained. Even some "Christmas" music works (for example, "Joy to the World"). Hymns involving the Holy Spirit are as fitting here as at Pentecost. Special music for this feast is also appearing, for example in the Liturgy of the Hours. A special favorite of mine is "The Baptism of Jesus" by F. Pratt Green, and the most recent edition of the

Worship hymnal has a fine meditation on the feast in "When John Baptized by Jordan's River" by Dudley Smith—both in familiar meters.

The most appropriate ritual would be a renewal of baptismal promises and communal sprinkling as is done at Easter. There have been objections to using this gesture at other times than Easter since a solemn covenant renewal needs a period of communal preparation. Yet what is Advent? Moreover, any community that regularly celebrates Infant Baptism as part of Sunday Eucharist will be familiar with public renewal of baptismal promises. The water sprinkling can also introduce the Eucharist on any Sunday. Linking those two elements in a single rite two or three times a year on the Baptism, Easter, and Pentecost does not overdo the gesture but rather enhances connections that might otherwise be missed.

In the following rite, the invitation is composed as an attempt to integrate Christmas, Epiphany, and the Baptism as progressive unfoldings of a single mystery at work within Jesus and within us. Just as the promises given at Pentecost are adapted from the version found in the confirmation rite that emphasizes the role of the Spirit, so these too are an adaptation to the winter festivals. In a similar way, the water blessing has been seasonally adapted from one of the introductory water blessings in the Roman sacramentary.

To avoid overloading the rite with too many presidential words, a communal acclamation can be introduced into the blessing. (The Rite for Infant Baptism, 223-4, suggests such an adaptation.) Some brief acclamation of praise with which the community is familiar works well. From my experience, having the musicians play quietly behind the presider's proclamation both unifies the verbal/aural event and makes the lead-in for the community acclamation much more smooth.

It is crucial to be both generous and playful with the actual sprinkling of water. Not a little pot but a bowl that only an adult could carry is needed to hold enough water to help a community experience the reality of Baptism once again. A bit of holly bound into the sprinkling branches with florist's tape will help keep the seasonal feel.

This feast is also one of the Sundays most suitable for Infant Baptism. The usual Baptismal sequence could be adapted by substituting some of the proper texts in the accompanying rite as alternatives.

Sequence with Infant Baptism

The letters (A), (B) and (B alternate), (C), and (D) indicate the appropriate substitutes from the sprinkling rite.

1. The Blessing of Water (B alternate)
2. The Instruction to Parents
3. The Baptismal Promises (A)
4. The Baptism
5. The Explanatory Rites
 Chrismation
 Clothing with White Garment
 Presentation of Lighted Candle
6. The Sprinkling (C)
7. The Instruction before Eucharist (D)

The rite could also be adapted for adult Baptism or reception into full communion.

Sequence of Adult Baptism/Profession of Faith and Confirmation

1. The Blessing of Water
  with Baptism (B alternate)
  with only Profession (B)
2. The Instruction to Candidates
3. The Promises (A)
4. The Reception into Full Communion
5. The Baptism
6. The Explanatory Rites
  White Garment
  Presentation of the Candle
7. The Confirmation
8. The Sprinkling (C)
9. The Instruction before the Eucharist (D)

In conclusion, I would suggest that the current Roman Catholic calendar needs to revise the computation of this festival. When Epiphany is celebrated on January 7 or 8, the Baptism of the Lord is simply observed on the following Monday. I would propose two ways of returning this feast to Sunday in such years. Either we follow the practice of the Anglican Church of Canada, for example, and celebrate the Epiphany even on January 1, or we substitute the Baptism for the texts of the Second Sunday in Ordinary Time. Chosen to emphasize more epiphanic material before the semi-continuous readings of Ordinary Time begin, this Sunday's Johannine selections are already an interruption of the gospel sequence. (The Year A selection is a second retelling of the Baptism of Jesus.) Their omission would not disturb the sequential gospel and would restore the Baptism-event to its deserved prominence.

THE RENEWAL OF BAPTISMAL PROMISES ON THE BAPTISM OF THE LORD

After the Homily the presbyter and other concelebrants who are to lead the rite go to the small table with bowl and branch prepared to the side of the sanctuary opposite the lectern. Facing the congregation, one of them invites everyone to stand. One of them then addresses the community in these or similar words:

The Invitation

PC/ACC:
My brothers and sisters,
for the last few weeks we have been celebrating
the birth of Emmanuel, God-with-us.
With the shepherds we have heard the Good News
of a new age dawning with peace for humankind.
With the Magi we have journeyed
by the light of faith to Bethlehem,
and found there our Saviour, God, and King.
With Mary we have pondered these things
in our hearts.

Now we celebrate the fulfillment of this mystery,
for today at Jesus's Baptism
the Spirit has proclaimed him as Messiah:
as the Priest who would give himself in sacrifice,
as the Prophet who would reveal God's presence
in word and sign,
as the King who would begin his reign on the cross.

We too in our Baptism have been anointed
by the Spirit
and have received a similar commission.
If you are willing to commit yourself anew
to our common task
of building God's kingdom in our day,
I ask you to respond: Yes, I do believe!
to each of the following questions.

The Promises (A)

PC/ACC:
Do you believe in God, our almighty Father,
who formed us from the earth
and breathed his life into us,
and who has called us to new life
in the water of Baptism
and by the fire of his Spirit?

ALL: Yes, I do believe!

PC/ACC:
Do you believe in Jesus, God's eternal Word,
who was born in human flesh of the Virgin Mary,
and at the Jordan was anointed
by the Holy Spirit as Messiah,
who by his death and rising has brought us over
into God's kingdom,
and who will come again in final, lasting glory?

ALL: Yes, I do believe!

PC/ACC:
Do you believe in the Holy Spirit,

who has anointed us too in Baptism
as God's holy people,
sent to proclaim his kingdom of justice and love,
of freedom and peace,
today and until the end of time?

ALL: Yes, I do believe!

PC/ACC:
Do you believe in yourselves, the Church,
living Christ's life in our world today,
one with the saints of ages past and yet to come,
and heirs to the promise of eternal life
with God and with his faithful forever?

ALL: Yes, I do believe!

*A presbyter then extends his hand over the bowl
and proclaims this Blessing.*

The Blessing of the Water (B)

ALL: (Acclamation)

PC/ACC:
Lord and Father,
in every age you have made water
a sign of your presence.
In the beginning
your Spirit brooded over the waters,
and so they became the source of all creation,
of all that life
which you loved and called very good.
Your chosen people passed through the waters

to reach their new land of freedom and peace.
With water your prophets announced
a new covenant you would make with humankind.

ALL: (Acclamation)

By water, made holy by Christ in the Jordan,
you transform our sinful nature
by the bath that gives rebirth.
Bless this water today;
let it remind us of our own Baptism.
Let the Spirit descend anew
upon all on whom it shall be sprinkled.

ALL: (Acclamation)

May the Spirit give us the power
to live daily as your devoted servants,
as your beloved sons and daughters,
till we come at last to our full glory
in your unending kingdom.

ALL: (Acclamation)

We ask this through Jesus the Messiah,
by the power of the Spirit moving us to pray.
Praise be yours forever and ever!

ALL: (sing) Amen! Amen! Amen!

A presbyter then addresses the community.

The Sprinkling (C)

PC/ACC: God has truly given us new birth by water and the Spirit. Let us relive the water through which we came to our new life. God will keep us faithful to our Lord Jesus and will bring us at last to share forever in his glory.

An acolyte carries the bowl and a presbyter sprinkles the whole community while everyone sings F. Pratt Green's "The Baptism of Jesus" or a similar song. When the sprinkling and singing are finished, the PC addresses the community from the presbyters' bench.

Instruction Before the Eucharist (D)

PC/ACC:
Dear friends,
we have relived God's call and our adoption
as his beloved sons and daughters in the Church.
Upon each of us some gift of the Spirit has come.
Now, as one united Body,
let us prepare to celebrate our Eucharist.

The Presentation of the Gifts begins immediately.

THE BLESSING OF
THE WATER FOR BAPTISM
(B alternate)

The Invitation

*After the Homily a presbyter or deacon goes to
stand by the font and faces the congregation.*

PC/ACC:
My dear brothers and sisters,
let us now ask God to bless this water
and to give this child/these children/the elect
new life in the Spirit.
Let us stand in prayer.

*As the presider pauses, a presbyter or deacon ex-
tends his hand over the font, proclaiming this Blessing.*

The Blessing

ALL: (Acclamation)

PC/ACC:
Lord and Father,
in every age you have made water
a sign of your presence.
In the beginning
your Spirit brooded over the waters,
and so they became the source of all creation,
of all that life
which you loved and called very good.

Your chosen people passed through the waters
to reach their new land of freedom and peace.
With water your prophets announced
a new covenant you would make with humankind.

ALL: (Acclamation)

PC/ACC:
By water,
made holy by Christ in the Jordan,
you transform our sinful nature
by the bath that gives rebirth.
Bless this water today +;
let the Spirit descend upon it
and upon all who shall be baptized here.
And let the Spirit descend anew
upon all whom it shall be sprinkled.

ALL: (Acclamation)

PC.ACC:
In that Spirit may we have the power
to live daily as your devoted servants,
as your beloved sons and daughters,
till we come at last to our full glory
in your unending kingdom.

ALL: (Acclamation)

PC/ACC:
We ask this through Jesus the Messiah,
by the power of the Spirit moving us to pray.
Praise be yours forever and ever!

ALL: (sing) Amen! Amen! Amen!

SPRING CYCLE

Ash Wednesday

Judging by the number of people who show up for church, Ash Wednesday is one of the most popular celebrations of the liturgical year. Whatever their reasons, Catholics are attached to "receiving ashes." The potential for communal worship is there.

Yet having gotten them to church, we don't seem to know what to do with them. The official service is minimal. The readings are brief (which might be good on a crowded schedule, but does every service have to be a full Eucharist?). Concerned primarily with *inner* conversion, they make no mention of Baptism and deal only in passing with the paschal mystery or the social dimension of sin and reconciliation.

The actual blessing of ashes consists of a brief invitation and a collect. There is no call to conversion other than the alternate distribution formula, no exploration of the areas in need of conversion except as developed by the homilist. Nor is there any physical participation by the community other than a single "Amen" and (not insignificantly) the presentation of a body to be marked with ashes.

To overcome some of these difficulties, different communities to which I belong have developed alternatives. The following complete service of blessing and distribution is a composite of several efforts, revised over time and intended for a predominantly adult community. The invitation to prayer has been expanded into a longer instruction, the collect transformed into a *berakhah* similar to those used at other solemn blessings in the Roman tradition (e.g., the Exsultet). A litany of repentance based on the *Book of Common Prayer*'s Litany of Penitence has been adapted as a communal examination of conscience that can easily be adjusted to the needs of a particular year.

Lastly, the distribution formula has been turned into a question evoking a verbal response. The current sacramentary's version both in diction and rhythm seems weak compared to the provisional sacramentary's text. "Sin" and "Gospel" are churchy; "faithful" and "Gospel" are singsong. "Live the Good News!" is a verbal and aural challenge.

THE BLESSING AND DISTRIBUTION OF ASHES

Immediately after the homily, a presbyter (and concelebrants) goes to stand behind the altar or table holding the ashes and addresses the community in these or similar words.

The Invitation

PC/ACC: Brothers and sisters, we have come here to recall who we are—a people baptized into Jesus Christ, but a people who have not fully lived the life of Jesus.

And so we are here to be called again by the all-powerful Word of God to a change of heart and a living of God's Good News.

If we are faithful to God's call, we shall be ready in six weeks to stand up with our catechumens and candidates and profess again our Easter faith.

To hear that call more clearly, let us examine our lives in the light of the Gospel.

Let us all kneel in prayer.

The Litany is read by a reader from the lectern. The pause for meditation at the indicated places should be lengthy.

The Litany of Repentance

CANTOR: Lord, have mercy!
(Or a similar refrain)

READER: Jesus, we have not loved you with our whole heart, and mind, and strength...and so we sing/cry out to you:

ALL: Lord, have mercy!

READER: Jesus, we have not come to you often enough in prayer, but have been busy about too many things...and so we sing/cry out to you:

ALL: Lord, have mercy!

READER: Jesus, we have been self-indulgent, loving our own comforts and careers and satisfactions too much...and so we sing/cry out to you:

ALL: Lord, have mercy!

READER: Jesus, we have not seen and loved you in our brothers and sisters, but have been blind to human need and suffering, indifferent to injustice and cruelty...and so we sing/cry out to you:

ALL: Lord, have mercy!

READER: Jesus, we have made idols of money, education, color, class, position...and have been prejudiced and contemptuous of anyone different from ourselves...and so we sing/cry out to you:

ALL: Lord, have mercy!

READER: Jesus, we have not seen and loved you present throughout your creation, but have wasted and polluted, and have ignored those who will come after us...and so we sing/cry out to you:

ALL: Lord, have mercy!

READER: Jesus, we turn to you...and we sing/cry out to you:

ALL: Lord, have mercy!

A presbyter stands and concludes the Litany with the following blessing.

The Blessing of the Ashes

PC/ACC:
Father, we acknowledge our need
to change our hearts and turn to you again.
We were buried with Christ in Baptism,
dying to sin, rising with him to new life.
Yet the power of your love
is still not fully revealed in us and in our world.

Father, bless these ashes +
and us who receive them.
May this signing with ashes
mark a new commitment of ourselves to you.
With Jesus may we accept the disappointments,
the burdens, the sufferings of this life—and
find them transformed by your Spirit.

At last, at the end of Lent, may we be ready
to celebrate Christ's passion with joy,
and on the day of resurrection
to rejoice forever with Jesus our Lord.

Through him you are blessed and praised,
almighty Father, in the unity of the Holy Spirit,
now and forever and ever.

ALL: (sing) Amen. Amen. Amen.

The Distribution

*The presbyter who proclaimed the blessing now
marks the first of the distributors with ashes and is
in turn marked himself. He then marks the others
who go immediately to the usual communion stations to mark the community.*

Alternate Formula

DISTRIBUTOR: Will you change your heart and
live the Good News?

RECIPIENT: I will.

Sacramentary Formula

DISTRIBUTOR: Will you turn away from sin and
be faithful to the Gospel?

RECIPIENT: I will.

*During the distribution there is appropriate mu-
sic, either instrumental or vocal or a combination.
After the distribution is finished, a presbyter gives
the following instruction.*

Instruction before the Eucharist

ACC/PC: We have proclaimed our sinfulness and our desire to repent. Let us now unite ourselves with Christ in this Eucharist. Here we shall find the power to carry out our resolve and to live anew in the Spirit.

The Presentation of Gifts follows immediately.

AN ALTERNATE BLESSING OF ASHES

Though there is a great deal of participation by word and gesture for the whole community in this composite service, adapting it for use with young people can be difficult. Group examination of conscience, for instance, is not easy for fidgeting youngsters. The following blessing uses the elements of the alternative service in a more compact form. The *berakhah* structure is retained in somewhat simpler language, filled with images and emotive words but broken up by communal dialogue and acclamation.

The combination of spoken and sung elements into one refrain is unusual but in practice has been effective. The spoken portion focuses everyone's attention on the significance of the material object and gesture; the sung portion becomes almost a mantra, unfocusing attention. If necessary, the sung portion can be omitted, but it is probably worth even an *a cappella* attempt.

Two-Part Refrain

ALL (*sing*):

We praise you, O Lord, for all your works are wonderful.

We praise you, O Lord, forever is your love.
(*Glory and Praise* #154)

PRESIDER:
Father, we are yours.
You made us from the dust of the earth, then
made us in Baptism your very own children.
Everything we are is your gift!

ALL: (*sing two-part refrain*)

PRESIDER:
Father, we are yours.
You sent your own Son Jesus to be one of us,
to be as human as we are.
He enjoyed parties and cried at the death of a
friend.
He loved little children
and became angry at injustice.
He showed us how good it is to be human!

ALL: (*sing two-part refrain*)

PRESIDER:
Father, we are yours.
By his suffering Jesus can end our fears.
By his death Jesus can destroy our selfishness.
By his resurrection Jesus can bring us to real
love—
love for each other and for you!

ALL: (*sing two-part refrain*)

PRESIDER:
We do praise You for your powerful love and
for the new and wonderful things you are
doing within us.
We praise You and thank You

in the name of Jesus and in the power of the
Holy Spirit,
now and forever and ever!

ALL: (*sing two-part refrain*)

PRESIDER: God, bless these ashes; make them a
sign of your love.

**ALL: God, bless these ashes; make them a
sign of your love.**

ALL: (*sing two-part refrain*)

A final observation: it is easy in special services to overdo music. Singing the Litany of Repentance and during the distribution and during the Presentation (at a full Eucharist) can exhaust a community. Many options are available: instrumental music, a soloist or choir selection, even silence (without the presider jumping in with the "Blessed are you..." prayers of the Presentation). A sense of balance is essential to create for our worshiping communities the proper milieu to begin their recommitment to baptismal life in Christ.

Rites of
Adult Initiation

The process of conversion is in a period of rapid flux in this country. Since the publication in English of the Rite for the Christian Initiation of Adults (RCIA) in 1975, American Catholics on various institutional levels have been attempting to understand and to implement the revisions proposed by that document. Use of the rites contained there still differs widely not only between dioceses but even from parish to neighboring parish; that diversity is a sign of health to me. The use of these new rites requires not merely a new form of liturgical finesse but a willingness to deal in a new way with the momentous process of becoming a Catholic Christian. The number of articles, publications, and programs indicates that valiant attempts are being made to meet that challenge; training sessions are nationally available; networking has begun. National implementation has been mandated by the bishops.

In this ongoing process, certain features of the RCIA seem already to have been readily accepted. The involvement of lay catechists, the "convert class" as a sharing group rather than as a merely instructional tool, and the active role of sponsors are three of the more obvious changes in our previous methods of catechizing those who wish to become Catholic Christians. Our dialogue with the program for conversion proposed by the RCIA, though well begun, is not complete. On the one hand, there are certain elements within the RCIA, certain presuppositions that it makes, that I think we are not yet facing; on the other, there are certain adaptations that I feel we shall have to make in its program for catechesis if we are to be faithful to our own experience.

The first of the RCIA's presuppositions that we have not always accepted is that sacraments and sacramentals make a difference. Perhaps part of the reason lies in our too frequent exposure to liturgy done badly; perhaps part comes from our immersion in a Protestant culture that in this country has tended to subordinate Sacrament to Word; still, we as American Catholics too often seem not to expect anything to *happen* in a ceremony. For many of us, a service seems to be an occasion, like a social gathering, not an event charged with significance both human and divine.

I am not trying to argue here from some *ex opere operato* theory of sacramentality; rather, I am speaking from my own experience and from that of friends who have at various times been not only touched but moved and transformed by a ritual. Burying a parent, vowing marriage, making religious profession, have all been "performative utterances," rituals by which *new* feelings have been evoked, *new* identities created.

Some programs for the catechumenate, however adept at employing the best techniques of both learning and communication theory, still seem to be structured in isolation from those liturgical celebrations that in the patristic period were *the* substance of the period of conversion. The root of this fragmentation might lie in the definition of conversion, which is at work in the back of our consciousness. However sophisticated our instructional techniques and theological content become, if we deep down are still defining "coming to faith" as learning the content of dogmas, then all we will ever expect the rites of initiation to be are periodic "nice" ceremonies. If we define conversion, though, not only as an intellectual process but as one involving the "total" person, then we will expect that the rites will be both deeply human, marked with warmth, compassion, and authentic personal contact, and truly divine, filled with prayerfulness and a sense of the presence of God's Spirit.

Some programs do focus upon the lectionary and the liturgy as *the* catechetical tool. Especially during the period of enlightenment during Lent, using the Johannine gospels of the A cycle as the basis both for weekly gatherings and for the texts of the scrutinies is a radical departure from the over-academic endeavors of the past. The challenge still lies in making the actual ritual as involving and as powerful as possible. Then sacramentality will *make* a difference.

Another aspect of taking sacraments and sacramentals seriously is the respect we need for the sacramental life of another Christian communion and also for the Holy Spirit, who works through them as well as through us. The RCIA suggests that the period of initiation into full communion with the Roman Catholic Church for those already baptized should be made holy by liturgical actions, yet it also warns against acting as if they were nonbaptized.[1] For excellent pastoral reasons, both the nonbaptized and the already baptized may be formed into a single group to prepare for initiation: the group dynamics make that especially important. But, to present the extreme case, for someone baptized, confirmed, and a regular communicant within the Episcopal Church to be signed with the Cross as if he or she had never belonged to Christ, or to be exorcised as if the Spirit did not already dwell within, both insults another Christian church and is completely insensitive to spiritual realities. Liturgy must begin with human *and* divine reality if it is ever to be authentic.

This distinction is made quite clear in the new American additions to the RCIA. In fact, they seem to make too sharp a division between those already baptized and those not. Both groups are on similar journeys of incorporation into the Catholic community; both need ritual to facilitate that incorporation. To keep them on separate liturgical tracks destroys their companionship on the journey.

Though adaptation has occurred in these two aspects of sacramentality, they remain challenges that the RCIA makes to the understanding and practice of the catechumenate in the American Catholic Church.

The RCIA's contents must be still further adapted to local traditions in order to have their optimal effect. On the national level, the American additions are a tribute to the sensitivity and creativity of those active in this field. Yet there are some questions that my personal experience and reflection say have not yet been successfully answered. Is the liturgy *as presently structured* in the RCIA the best tool for helping Americans become Catholics? Is there something inauthentic about even the new American RCIA's approach?

In order to understand the overall program for liturgy proposed by the RCIA, let us begin with a schematic overview of the public and semi-public rites, in which both the baptized and nonbaptized and the parish community could participate. (See Table 1.)

Both from viewing them as a whole and from experiencing some of them individually for several years, I find three major criticisms I would make of these rites. First is the overwhelming predominance of word over gesture. Though each service contains some action, too often it is quite minimal, as in the laying on of hands for the Scrutinies. The Presentations are nothing but words, or possibly the handing over of a book or text. If we are trying to facilitate the conversion not of minds but of persons, we must become more sensory in our modes of ritual communication.

There have been attempts to become more tactile. In many places, for example, the sponsors make *big* signs of the cross during the making of catechumens or during the ephphetha. Or they mark the eyes of the elect on the Sunday of the man born blind. Though most encouraging, this use of gesture needs to be expanded and to be officially recognized.

117

PART ONE: Festival Seasons (Spring Cycle)

Some Sunday	Lent I	Lent II	Lent III	During Week III	Lent IV	During Week IV	Lent V	Holy Saturday
First Promise, Signing with the Cross, and Welcome	Election and Enrollment	Penitential Rite for Candidates	First Scrutiny	Presentation of the Creed	Second Scrutiny	Presentation of the Lord's Prayer	Third Scrutiny	Various rites, especially Anointing with Oil of Catechumens
Becoming a catechumen or a candidate	Proximate preparation		Exorcism	Preparation for the Profession of Faith	Exorcism	Meaning of Christian prayer	Exorcism	Final preparation

The second of my criticisms is the minimal participation of the gathered community in these rites. In the entire series, the faithful are asked to respond to only one question; otherwise, except for answering the calls to silent prayer and interjecting an occasional "Amen," their experience is reduced to watching an official minister say words over people. The ecclesiology springing from Vatican II and our own liturgical growth in this country in the last decades clearly necessitate some revision of this truncated sharing.

Lastly and perhaps most significantly, this series of rites also seems to presume that we are dealing with really wicked people. The emphasis upon sin and the influence of the devil is a bit overwhelming. Some modifications have already been made: the ancient exorcisms, especially in the Scrutinies, were imprecatory in character, addressing the devil directly; those in the RCIA are deprecatory, addressing God about the devil.[2] Though stylistically less impressive, this change seems to reveal an awareness of the difference between being enmeshed in the power of evil in this world and actual demonic possession. Yet more adaptation still seems necessary.

In the ancient world and in many mission lands, the stronger emphasis was and possibly remains essential; for most of the initiates I have known, even the current tone is inaccurate and inauthentic. In modern America most people know a great deal about Jesus, and a great many are sincerely trying to follow him. What they require is an adaptation that is less purification and more enlightenment. Without denying the reality of sinfulness, they need to be called through ritual to lay aside an older self by becoming a new person in Jesus and assuming a new identity within his community.[3] Such ritual elements are present in the existing rites but require alteration and re-emphasis to play a more complete role.

To examine certain of the services in detail, let us begin with the rite that makes nonbaptized individuals catechumens by their First Promise and the communal Signing with the Cross. In its present form, I feel this ceremony is the most satisfying of the series. The words express a broad view of conversion; the central gesture of signing the Cross is a strong one *if* it is carried out in its multiple form with the marking of many different senses. (The American adaptations have added "hands" and "feet.") An expression of assent—which could be expanded—is required both of sponsors and of the catechumen; the whole community is questioned about its willingness to assume responsibility for this new member. Sponsors or a number of the faithful can also participate in the multiple signings. The total effect can thus be a vivid experience of a rite of passage for all involved. Following the suggestion of the RCIA,[4] we also need a similar rite of welcome for the already baptized by which the same sense of mutual commitment is created. I am not certain that the new American addition, which repeats the Signing of the Cross with different words, is a step in the right direction. The visual and dramatic message is too close to the entrance into the catechumenate. Would not a vigorous public handshake from the pastor similar to the "right hand of fellowship" in certain Protestant traditions be more appropriate?

To focus, though, on the final period of Enlightenment that coincides with Lent, this second-to-last stage is inaugurated in a rather moving service. The sponsors are publicly questioned, and those being initiated are asked to "sign up," a gesture particularly vivid in our culture. Sinfulness and moral conversion are not the dominant motif in this rite; the ceremony establishes instead, in a more intense way, who the initiates are within the community and where they are heading.

Lacking in the liturgy, though, is any active involvement of the community gathered for the service. Possibly asking once again for communal acceptance and for a promise of continued support as is done in the First Promise would begin to involve and challenge those assembled. Even a simple gesture like applause at the right moment would be effective (cf., page 63, "RCIA Winter Cycle").

In the remaining rites of the Enlightenment, I find evident the exaggerated moral emphasis I mentioned before. Since it is the Scrutinies that are intended for Sunday (i.e., communal celebration), while the Presentations are designated for mid-week—at best, semi-public—celebration, the exorcistic element becomes overwhelming, especially for the parish community. Adding the new Penitential Rite for those already baptized on Lent II makes this situation even worse. Now *four* successive Sundays are dominated by sinfulness and repentance.

Moreover, the Scrutinies and the Penitential Rite are the services with the least community participation and the most minimal use of gesture.

Moral conversion is an essential part of the total process: the triple Renunciation of Sin is the immediate prelude at Easter Vigil to the Profession of Faith. To prepare the community and the elect for that moment requires the celebration of one or two Scrutinies; but the rite needs enrichment. On Lent V, after the homily, the minister presiding could call the entire community to repentance, inaugurate some examination of conscience, and then lead in the General Confession.[5] The nonbaptized could publicly receive that Anointing with the Oil of Catechumens, which the RCIA regards as especially significant[6]; those already baptized could receive a laying on of hands with a formula taken from the day's Gospel. The exorcism or blessing from the appropriate Scrutiny could be the conclusion. Such a rite would be somewhat more sensory, definitely more communal, and adaptable for both kinds of initiates since different rituals would be carried out with each type (cf., page 63, "RCIA Winter Cycle").

To substitute for one of the Scrutinies, one of the Presentation rites could also be used for both kinds of initiates. Since the Presentation of the Creed symbolically prepares the initiates for their profession of faith at Easter Vigil, that ceremony could take place on Lent III instead of during the week following. The minister presiding could instruct the elect in the significance of what they are about to hear, and then lead the community in the recitation of the Creed while the elect listen in silence.[7] Prayer for the elect and some form of the Ephphetha could follow. The community could repeat the words of the Ephphetha formula after the presider while the sponsors mark the ears and the mouth. The exorcism or prayer from the Lent III Scrutiny would still be appropriate, especially those proper to Cycle A. Yet the dominant theme would not be simply sinfulness and moral conversion (cf., page 63, "RCIA Winter Cycle").

One possible objection is that members of a number of churches would have already learned and professed the Creed for years. Yet the point of the rite is that the Creed is heard and will later be professed in the context of the Catholic community. It is a symbolic statement that the already baptized also require.[8]

Another Sunday rite could also be developed out of the Presentation of the Lord's Prayer, or of the Gospels if that was not worked into the entry into the catechumenate. Or we could go outside the Roman tradition and wash the initiates' feet as is done in the Ambrosian baptismal ceremonies. The elect might learn more about the morality by which the members of the Church are supposed to live by that gesture than through any lecture, discussion, or counseling. Or we might decide that public rituals on Lent I, III, and V are adequate before the rich experience of Holy Week/Easter begins on Palm Sunday. Again, as the RCIA constantly reiterates, only sensitivity for and adaptation to local customs and circumstances can resolve such a question.

In sum, I have discussed certain challenges that the RCIA makes to our understanding and practice of sacramentality and some concrete areas in which we need to be creative with the RCIA's rites. I am not advocating that sin should be eliminated or that every Roman Catholic rite of initiation should suddenly acquire the frequent boisterousness of a charismatic prayer meeting; but human warmth, communal sharing, and authentic prayer can allow the Spirit to enter in and bring change. Sinners become saints, the ignorant are enlightened, the fearful are "clothed with power from on high." Human beings fully alive become the images of the living Jesus.

NOTES

[1] *Rite of the Christian Initiation of Adults*, sections 295-305, contained in the *Rites of the Catholic Church* 1 (New York: Pueblo Publishing Co., 1976).

[2] Balthasar Fischer, "Baptismal exorcism in the Catholic Baptismal Rites after Vatican II," *Studia Liturgica* 10, no. 1, 53-55; and *Rite of Christain Initiation of Adults (Study Edition)* (Chicago: Liturgy Training Publications, 1988).

Michel Dujarier, *The Rites of Christian Initiation* (New York: William H. Sadlier, Inc., 1979), 128. Dujarier disagrees on this point but seems not to have made Fischer's distinction.

[3] Roger Beraudy, S.S., "Scrutinies and Exorcisms," *Adult Baptism and the Catechumenate*, ed. Johannes Wagner, Concilium Series 22 (New York: Paulist Press, 1967), 57-61.

[4] RCIA, old 300, new 405.

[5] RCIA, old 254, new 350.

[6] RCIA, old 127-129, new 98-101.

[7] RCIA, old 186, new 160.

[8] RCIA, old 302, new 407. Also, National Statutes on the Catechumenate, #31.

Palm Sunday and Easter Triduum

Palm Sunday

Here is a very odd fact to relate: the parish I belong to has scheduled a full-scale, outdoor, communal Palm Sunday parade/procession annually since 1975—and we have never canceled because of inclement weather. The most eerie experience was in 1984. The morning-long rain stopped at 10:30. The sun broke through with the first trumpet call at 11:00. And the downpour began again five minutes after the last person marched in the front door. Clearly God wants us to try.

This parade is quite popular. It has color and music and a sense of spring about it. As good liturgy, though, it has something for everyone to *do*. Children can carry the small-size banners; adults can carry the bigger ones and the censers. Most people can sing; most people can walk. Even the aged and infirm who can't march say that the parade is still a prayerful experience as they wait in church for the rest of the community to arrive. As a dear friend once remarked, she felt as if she was waiting for the rest of us to catch up with her on the journey to the New Jerusalem.

What helps enhance the parade is the use of bells. Palms and banners are visual; the bells are an additional aural stimulus that bonds the marchers together. Since everyone brings their own from home, there is a strong sense of ownership. Little kids in their parents' arms may not sing, but they love to make noise with their bells.

The major hurdle to such a parade is the singing. We walk six abreast so there is mutual support. Two trumpeters placed in the middle of the route keep both front and rear relatively together. Yet the three stanzas of "All Glory, Praise, and Honor" wear thin on the fifth repetition. Changing songs in the middle seems too difficult. And so we have written three additional stanzas: two based upon Psalm 72 and one upon the Gospel narrative of the Entry. In most years two or two-and-one-half repetitions allow 400 people to march 150 yards and into their places in church.

Even for those celebrations that use the Solemn Entrance format, the additional verses offer creative possibilities. The instrumentation for the stanzas can more easily differ; various portions of the community can alternate singing; different portions of the entrance procession can move during different stanzas. Six stanzas do provide much more space for creativity to work.

With a little effort at community involvement, the celebration of Palm Sunday can be a moving introduction to the paschal celebration! With delight for ear and eye, how can anyone miss the message that a special time has come—the time to relive *the* story in a special and deeper way.

ALL GLORY

All glory, praise, and honor
To you, Redeemer King!
To whom the lips of children
Made glad hosannas ring.
You are the King of Israel
And David's royal Son,
Who in the Lord's name comes now,
Our King and Blessed One.
The prophets had proclaimed you
A royal son to be,
A just and righteous ruler
Whose reign reached sea to sea.
As son you rule forever,
Your blessings never cease;
Your days would be remembered
For virtue, joy, and peace.
The poor would call upon you,
The hungry you would feed;
The suff'ring you would comfort,
The wand'ring you would lead;
The mountains, hills, and valleys
Would echo with your praise;
The orchards, fields, the lakes and streams
Would thrive through endless days.
Our sin, our death, our sadness
Are set beneath your feet:
You crush them like the branches
Bestrewn upon the street.
Exultant we cry out to you
And lift our joyful psalm:
Victorious are you on this day
And through all time to come.

The company of angels
Now sings your praise on high;
All humankind and all things
Created make reply.
The people of the Hebrews
With palms before you went;
Our praise and prayer and anthems
Before you we present.
To you before your passion
They sang their hymns of praise;
To you, now high exalted,
Our melody we raise.
You did accept their praises;
Accept the prayers we bring,
For you rejoice in every good,
Our good and gracious King!

Easter Triduum

Holy Thursday

For older Catholics raised in the eucharistic piety of the pre-Vatican II period, the beginning of the Triduum evokes strong memories. Elaborate ceremonial reminiscent of Corpus Christi and Forty Hours, singing the Gloria, ringing bells, watching Christ move among his people—all were the prelude to the long hours of personal watch by the repository. If good liturgy means popular involvement, the Holy Thursday celebrations of thirty years ago were a real success.

Much of the piety and ceremonial that marked those celebrations has gone. And what has replaced it? I have a suspicion that Holy Thursday has become the most uprooted and therefore incoherent service within the entire spring cycle.

The 1970 lectionary at first glance gives some rootedness, some sense of coherence, to the story we are called to remember this night. The first reading from Exodus 12 concerns the directions for preparing and eating the passover meal and seems to explain the reason for Jesus' gathering with his disciples. The epistle from 1 Corinthians 11 gives Paul's institution narrative and shows how Jesus transformed that pass-over rite. The gospel from John 13 helps unravel the meaning of the Eucharist by describing the humility of the master of the feast. The conclusion is obvious: we are somehow Christianizing a Jewish celebration or are celebrating that passover ourselves.

Various communities have heard that message and have adapted their services accordingly. Families at home or whole parishes are invited to sit seder before the Eucharist. Seder elements such as the Four Questions or the matzoh are introduced into the service itself. Pastoral staffs wash feet.

I would suggest, though, that these adaptations are ultimately as far removed from the Scriptures and the original Roman liturgical tradition as the Corpus Christi-like services they are trying to replace. And responsibility for that scriptural incoherence lies with the creators of the revised lectionary, who created an artificial linkage by their selection.

A brief consideration of liturgical history may help make my suggestion clear. The original celebration of the Triduum consisted of a two-day fast ending in the all-night vigil. That the vigil was early understood in terms of the Passover feast is clear in several ways. In Greek and in the Romance languages, for instance, the word for "Easter" *is* the word for "Passover." The earliest vigil lectionaries all include Exodus 15, the crossing of the Red Sea. Texts such as the Exsultet are filled with passover imagery. The opening Instruction added by the post-Vatican II revisers remained true to this tradition: "On this most holy night, when our Lord Jesus passed from death to life,...is the passover of the Lord."

As the Thursday and Friday services were added, the chronology implicit in them was not synoptic but Johannine. John's Passion on Good Friday presents us with the sacrifice of the true passover lamb. John even quotes Exodus 12, insisting that Jesus' legs were not broken. John's footwashing narrative on Holy Thursday begins "before the festival of Passover" and goes on to describe a Last Supper that is not a seder but focuses instead upon an ablution ritual.

In the Roman tradition, Exodus 12 was read either at the Vigil or on Good Friday (or in both services). Nor was the former epistle for Holy Thursday the pruned-down Pauline institution narrative but the full context of Chapter 11, wherein Paul describes the mutual sensitivity and love that are the prerequuisite to the valid celebration of the common meal.

I am not suggesting here that there is anything wrong with the synoptic tradition or its chronology or that it could not be used as the basis for celebrating the Triduum. However, I do think we do good liturgy a disservice when we try to lay a foreign perspective upon a scriptural and liturgical tradition.

To summarize, what is Holy Thursday *not?* It is not Corpus Christi. I like damask drapes, Glorias, white vestments, and lots of bell-ringing and incense; but I think those belong with the climax of the Triduum, the Easter Vigil. Holy Thursday is not a seder; if there is a Christianized passover meal, it is the Easter Vigil.

Nor is Holy Thursday a festival of transubstantiation: the Lord's command is to eat and drink in his memory, not to gaze and ponder. Nor is it a festival of the priesthood: to say that Jesus "ordained" the apostles at the Last Supper is a highly derivative theological statement. The Lord's commandment in Paul is addressed to the community and insists that *all* should eat *and* drink. Nor is it a festival of official ministry. Jesus was not addressing the pastoral staff (ordained or not); the Lord's command in John is addressed to all his disciples.

What are we left with? I would suggest that we are left with a service that is subdued and restrained. We are left with stories of humility and reconciliation. We are entering into the paschal mystery through the door of mutual acceptance and service. On Good Friday we will discover the depth of our commitment as we venerate the cross. At last at the Vigil we shall exuberantly celebrate the glory in which that mystery gives us a share. But Holy Thursday is only the door.

How do we act that out in liturgy? The fulfillment of the Lord's command that all should eat and drink is familiar to us from our Sunday worship. Eucharistic Prayer for Reconciliation I, perhaps omitting some of the passover references, contains very appropriate eucharistic words for this service.

How is the community to act out the other command of the Lord this night? After initial resistance, I have come to love the custom of involving the entire community in washing hands. To insist upon *foot*washing is probably to confuse the message and the medium. To insist on footwashing means that time considerations will make most people spectators whenever the community numbers more than one hundred. With hand washing the number of available tables, basins, pitchers, and towels is the only restriction on the community's involvement (One station = fifty people = twenty minutes). The following service has evolved through use both in small groups such as faculty retreats and in large parish celebrations. It flows quite easily. The special role of official ministry within the community can be recognized if a member of the pastoral staff begins the rite at each station by washing someone else's hands and then coming up last at that station to have his or her hands washed. Thus all serve and are served, and we are bound together in our journey to glory.

THE COMMITMENT TO SERVICE AND EXCHANGE OF PEACE

Before the service several stations are prepared at places chosen beforehand. At each station there is a table covered with a cloth, and resting on the table are a large bowl or basin, a pitcher filled with water, and a towel.

After the homily the PC goes to the head of the main aisle and addresses the community:

PC: In Jesus' washing the feet of his disciples, we recognize his command to serve one another all of our lives and to let others serve us in loving friendship. To carry out that command tonight, let us all come forward and in mutual service wash each others' hands.

The PC and ACCs or members of the pastoral staff go to each of the stations and invite the first person in the appropriate pew to come forward. After washing and drying this person's hands, the CC or staff member returns to his or her place; the community continues the action, following an order similar to the communion procession.

The acolytes replenish the pitchers and change the towels when necessary.

When all are finished, the acolytes remove the towels and pitchers. The PC returns to the head of the main aisle and addresses the community:

ACC/PC: Would you all please stand.

PC: Now that we have acted out our commitment in gesture, I ask you to express your faith and commitment aloud by answering: "Yes, I am!" to the following questions.

Our Lord Jesus, after he had washed the feet of his disciples, asked them, "Do you understand what I have done to you?" Are you ready now to follow the Lord in service to one another?

ALL: Yes, I am!

PC: Our Lord Jesus said, "If you are bringing your offering to the altar, and there remember that your brother or sister has something against you, go and be reconciled with your brother or sister first, and then come back and present your offering."

Are you willing to be reconciled with your brothers and sisters so that we can all together present our gifts to the Lord?

ALL: Yes, I am!

PC: Our Lord Jesus said to his troubled friends, "Peace is my farewell to you!"

Are you able to know the Lord's peace, and to share it with one another?

ALL: Yes, I am!

PC: We are entering into the depth of the mystery of Jesus' death and resurrection, and we must enter this mystery together and unafraid.

The peace of the Lord Jesus be with you all!

ALL: And also with you!

ACC/PC: Let us share the Lord's peace with one another!

The PC, the ACCs, and others in the sanctuary should move among the community as well. After a time the PC returns to the presbyters' bench and addresses the community.

Instruction Before the Eucharist

PC: We have shared the peace of the Lord with one another. Now we must relive his complete surrender of himself in obedience to the Father—so that he could enter the fullness of life and share that life with us. By our sharing in his Body and Blood, Jesus makes us more truly one in himself.

The Preparation of the Altar and Gifts begins immediately.

Good Friday

The danger of historicizing the liturgy of the Easter Triduum is perhaps greatest on Good Friday. Liturgy becomes passion play. We hear about the cross being nailed together in the sanctuary during the proclamation of the Passion, and the veneration involving everyone coming up to pound in another nail. Is this to make certain everyone feels sufficiently guilty? This spring's new tale concerned the pastor who personally carried in a life-size cross from the vestibule—and stumbled and fell at each of the three stages of presentation. I can only wonder what the community was then asked to venerate.

Liturgy is not pretend. Jesus died on Good Friday; he is not dead today. We are not holding a wake for Jesus nor are we making reparation to him for his suffering. We need to take seriously the Johannine passion narrative, which is the choice of (almost) every liturgical tradition as the gospel passage for the day. In John, the cross is the beginning of Jesus' glorification. Lifted from the earth, he will draw all to himself. Through the Spirit that he hands over and the blood and water that flow from his side, the Church is given the sacraments of initiation to celebrate on Easter night.

The only death at this year's celebration of Good Friday is our own. We are confronted again with the full horror of the cross and are asked to reach out in faith and to take on its life-giving mystery as the pattern for our own life.

How do we find a visual representation, a icon for John's Passion? How do we proclaim the paradox: death and the beginning of victory? The most recent Catholic custom involved each worshiper kissing the feet of Jesus on the crucifix. Rooted in baroque piety, this gesture easily produced an emotional reaction because of the graphic gore of the image. Whether it called beyond to a deeper level of faith probably depended upon the worshiper. The difficulty with this custom is its focus upon something *objective,* the past sufferings of the historical Jesus, and not upon the living and present reality of the liturgical celebration.

To provide an alternative to such objectivity, many parishes now present a cross, not a crucifix, for veneration. Some of these crosses are utterly bare and larger than life; others are smaller and beautifully decorated in the tradition of the *crux gemmata.*

For years my parish has used a life-size cross made of two logs lashed together and attached to a stable base. From the beginning of the service it stands in the center of the sanctuary. At its foot the initial prostration occurs; around it the Passion is proclaimed.

The beginning of the veneration has become not the carrying in of the cross or its gradual unveiling. Adapting a Byzantine custom, we have fashioned out of vine a crown about fifteen inches in diameter, marked not by thorns but with red and white flowers. We begin by crowning the bare cross, usually in silence, followed immediately by the traditional threefold acclamation: "This is the wood of the Cross..." In words that try to capture the visual and the spiritual tension of the moment, the invitation to approach is extended to all:

PC: The body of the historical Jesus no longer hangs upon the Cross. The Cross is here so that the triumph that took place in Jesus once and for all might continue to happen in his Body—so that his triumph might take place in us, in our lives and in our death. In this hope, come and embrace the Cross.

For the next thirty minutes, everyone in the congregation of three hundred or so approaches one by one to venerate, while song and silence and scripture help interpret the event. It is the cross of Jesus; it is my cross; it is our cross; it is the beginning of glory. This is the proclamation of faith in which past and present, the objective and the personal, emotion and commitment, are interwoven into a complex whole. Without turning Good Friday into the Triumph of the Cross, a rich celebration can still mark this traditionally somber day if we find a way to represent John's Passion with artistry and with prayer.

Holy Saturday

One service within the rich sequence of the RCIA that does not seem to be much discussed (or performed?) is the semi-public gathering with the elect for prayer on Holy Saturday. A broad variety of possible words and gestures is provided (cf., RCIA old 193-207); yet that very variety presents a problem: What is appropriate and how long should the service be with the whole Vigil coming that night?

Some gathering of the elect happens on that day, though, since some sort of practice is needed. (Catechumenal rites are simple enough to be done effectively by practicing only with the sponsors; the full rites of initiation need at least basic blocking for everyone.) Beginning that rehearsal with a half-hour of common prayer involving elect, sponsors, catechists, clergy, musicians, and acolytes can be a effective prelude for the practice and for the Vigil itself.

The following rite is one attempt to pull the various possibilities into a dynamic whole. For coherence it has an opening Greeting and a concluding Blessing. The new RCIA moves in this direction with a concluding blessing and dismissal not found in the old rite. The recitation of the Creed is omitted since that will be part of the Vigil; instead the Ephphetha is expanded to prepare for that recitation.

After that strong tactile and verbal gesture, the scripture reading is taken from the selections given for the choice of a name. Since few Americans will choose a new name, explaining the neophytes' given names (as RCIA old 205, new 202 suggests) and presenting them with a card inscribed in calligraphy with their name, its derivation, and an appropriate scripture verse is quite moving.

This element can carry over into the first part of the common prayer by employing the names within a Litany of the Saints. The final prayer of Exorcism, adapted from the Minor Exorcisms, leads into the a laying-on of hands and dismissal.

Clear, coherent, highly sensuous, such an attempt at a pre-initiation service can be an effective prelude to the climax of the Lenten journey.

HOLY SATURDAY
PRE-INITIATION SERVICE

Items Needed:
red vestments
cards with names

When everyone has assembled in the small chapel, the elect should seat themselves in the center rows of chairs with their sponsors and godparents either behind or beside them. After informal introductions, the service begins.

Introduction

PC: In the name of the Father +, and of the Son, and of the Holy Spirit.

ALL: Amen.

The Lord be with you. *(Or one of the other Greetings)*

ALL: And also with you.

The PC welcomes everyone and gives an introduction to the service.

The Ephphetha

Turning to the elect, a presbyter addresses them in these or similar words:

PC/ACC:
N.&N., during these months of your preparation,
God has always been with you to guide you
and to lead you to a deeper knowledge and love
of himself and of the Church
that his Son established
by his death on the Cross.

As you prepare now
to become a full member of that Church,
never forget that it was God's free gift of grace
that first called you here,
God's grace that enabled you to hear
and understand his word,
God's grace that has given you the power
to change your life.

(*Addressing the community*)
Let us all pray that these elect might respond fully
to the call of God's grace. (*Pause.*)

Sponsors and godparents, I invite you now to
mark the elect with the sign of faith; and I invite
this whole community to repeat these words after
me.

PC/ACC should pause at the asterisks in the text.

(*On the ears*)
Christ opened the ears of the deaf.*
In his name we say to you:*
Ephphetha, be opened! +*
May you hear his call to faith.*

(*On the mouth*)
Christ opened the mouth of the dumb*
  and gave them speech.*
  In his name we say to you:*
Ephphetha, be opened! +*
  May you profess the faith you have heard*
  to the glory and praise of God.*

The Giving of Names

Scripture reading
One of the sponsors or godparents (RCIA old 204, new 201)

Instruction
One of the catechists

Explanation and Presentation of the Baptismal Names
Catechists and sponsors and godparents

Prayer and Exorcism
After the presentation of names, the PC/ACC addresses the community in these or similar words:

PC/ACC: United not only with God's people gathered here but with all the holy men and women of faith who have gone before us, let us entrust these elect to the love and care of the saints.

READER/CANTOR: The response is, **Pray for her/him/them!**

The reader or cantor proclaims the list of names, beginning with Mary and Joseph and other biblical saints and moving into the various patron saints of the elect (and of the sponsors and godparents). The concluding invocation is always the following:

All holy men and women, saints of God:

ALL: (Response)

PC/ACC: *(extending right hand over the elect)*
Father of all mercies,
you gave us your beloved Son
to rescue us from sin by the power of his Cross
and to give us the true freedom of your children.

Look now on N.&N.
They have experienced temptation
and know their human weakness.
Look on them with love
and fulfill their hope in your sight.
Search their inmost heart today,
and guard them
as they await the fullness of life in Jesus.
Bring to completion the plan of your love.
May they enter the fellowship of your Church
in the full glory of the resurrection.
We ask this through Christ our crucified Lord.

ALL: Amen.

The PC/ACC lays his hands on the heads of the elect and says to each:

PC/ACC:
N., may Jesus free you from your sins
and raise you to life,
for he is Lord forever and ever.

ALL: Amen!

Final Blessing

ACC/PC: Bow your heads and pray for God's blessing. (*Pause.*)

PC?ACC:
As the glory of Easter draws near,
may God fill us all with new strength and life;
in the name of the Father +,
and of the Son, and of the Holy Spirit.

ALL: Amen!

ACC/PC: Go in peace until we meet again this night.

Easter Vigil

The first of the many rich symbols that fill the Easter Vigil is getting progressively more difficult to create. With the increasing use of security lighting and sodium vapor lamps, the night has been turned into day before the new fire is ever lit. Even if the side courtyard or the parking lot lights can be doused, our church's main entrance fronts onto a street with photosensor lighting. We cannot gather outside in anything like darkness.

There are the additional difficulties: an outdoor gathering in unpredictable weather, candles extinguished by wind, the movement of large groups of people into a darkened building. It almost seems that God doesn't want us to try.

Yet we can gather in something like darkness inside the church. With some effort we can turn off not only the interior lights but sufficient exterior bulbs to create a striking effect. (The strategic use of rolls of black paper can help.)

What can be done to make more palpable this experience of sitting in darkness? One possibility is to have the community, including the clergy, gather in the almost darkened church. When the time to begin the service comes, the presider from his seat can give the opening Instruction. The last light is turned off, and everyone sits in silence for two or three minutes with no sensory stimulus except the sound of water trickling in the baptismal font.

The sudden leaping up and dying out of the fire in the vestibule shatters the night. The immediate entrance of the lighted, five-foot-tall Easter Candle borne aloft clearly proclaims Light's victory: one flame *can* illumine a whole building. And as that flame spreads throughout the whole community, the words of the Exsultet make sense.

> Rejoice, O Mother Church!...
> The risen Savior shines upon you!...
> Darkness vanishes forever!

Another possible adaptation is to give a guided meditation on the meaning of darkness. If there is only silence, the shuffling feet become distracting, and children grow restive. The sequence just described can be followed, inserting the following meditation between the dousing of the last light and the lighting of the fire. Experience has shown that the two readers' skill with their pencil flashlights is crucial. The sense of sitting in darkness can be destroyed if there is a winking off and on from the rear corners.

THE LIGHT SERVICE

The Meditation in Darkness

When all are seated, the PC enters and sits on the presbyters' bench. The readers of this Meditation should already be in place in the back corners with their pencil flashlights. The PC gives the opening Instruction to the community, and then the last lights are extinguished. After a moment's pause, the left reader begins. The readers must be careful that their flashlights do not shine off their pages and illuminate the church.

LEFT: Let us reflect on the darkness of ignorance and the darkness of selfishness. (*Pause.*)

RIGHT: Let us reflect on the darkness of loneliness and the darkness of discouragement. (*Pause.*)

LEFT: Let us reflect on the darkness of serious illness, illness of the body and illness of the mind. (*Pause.*)

RIGHT: Let us reflect on the darkness of oppression and the darkness of discrimination. (*Pause.*)

LEFT: Let us reflect on the darkness of hatred and the darkness of indifference. (*Pause.*)

RIGHT: Let us reflect on how we have chosen darkness and have refused to see light. (*Pause.*)

LEFT: But the light of Christ, rising in glory,

RIGHT: Dispels the darkness of our minds and hearts!

The readers then go to the vestibule if they are to help with the bringing in of the Easter Candle. Otherwise, they return to their places.

	A	B	C
creation	Genesis 1,1-2,2	Sirach 42,15-43,33	Genesis 2,5-10; 16-25
call	Isaiah 54,5-14	Genesis 22,1-18	Baruch 3,9-15; 3,29-4,4
liberation	Exodus 14,15-31; 15,20-21		
promise	Jeremiah 31,31-34	Ezechiel 37,1-14	Ezechiel 36,16-28
Baptism	Romans 6,3-11		

If there are no Baptisms, use the following:

	A	B	C
	Romans 6,3-11	Galatians 3,21-4,7	Colossians 2,6-13; 3,1-4

Resurrection & commission
(If there are no Baptisms, omit the verses in parentheses):

	A	B	C
	Matthew 28,1-10	Mark 16,1-8; (16-20)	Luke 24,1-12 (36:44-49)

Table 2.

As a final observation on the Service of Light, I disagree strongly with repositioning the Exsultet after the Resurrection Gospel. The whole story of salvation shared in the Scriptures of this night is read in the radiance of the Risen One. The proper response to that ages-long story is not the thanksgiving for light but the rites of initiation.

The Liturgy of the Word

Another element in the Easter Vigil that can present difficulties is the Liturgy of the Word. The core of "vigiling" has its roots in communities gathered to recall in an intense and explicit way that history that shaped their present identity and hopes for the future. Yet, how many readings should there be? Which ones should be chosen?

While researching an answer to such questions several years ago, I reached several conclusions (cf. "Trimming the Vigil Readings," *Liturgy* 25, no. 1 (Jan/Feb 1980), 29-32). First, the oldest Roman tradition was content with four Old Testament selections. Second, the oldest series also attempted to balance story and interpretation by alternating historical readings with prophetic selections. Lastly, as the series had expanded over the centuries from four to seven to twelve, a real thematic continuity remained at work.

From these conclusions I constructed a tentative three-year cycle using different selections with an underlying structure. (See Table 2.)

Certain comments from those who have used the schema have been helpful. The B Sirach reading needs to be shortened. The C Genesis reading needs careful translation so that the point of the Hebrew tale is not lost in the noninclusive use of the English "man." The extended Gospels are effective because the rites of initiation stand revealed as the Church's carrying out of the Lord's final command (cf. Blessing of the Baptismal Water.)

Giving a real shape to the readings themselves is just the beginning of the task. The choice of appropriate responsorial music and of prayers (and of visuals?) is equally as important in creating a total experience of worship.

The Eucharistic Prayer

Most of the explanatory rites associated with Baptism have a visual impact: white robes, flaming candles. One rite, chrismation, appeals to smell as much as to sight if the oil is properly perfumed. Yet the ancient world knew another explanatory gesture that appealed to taste: water and a mixture of honey and milk blessed during the Eucharistic Prayer and given to the neophytes to drink. Founded apparently upon Old Testament exodus imagery, this ritual enabled the neophytes at communion to literally taste and see the goodness of the Lord (cf., Ps 34:8).

Since the honey and milk seem to speak more powerfully, restoring at least that part of the gesture seems worthwhile. In Eucharistic Prayer III, for example, after the Memento for "all the people gathered here," the appropriate Memento should be added from among those given in the ritual Masses section of the sacramentary or from the RCIA old 391, new 242. The following blessing could then be added before we pray for "all (God's) children wherever they may be."

Bless for them this mixture of honey and
milk +,
Once you promised to our ancestors
that you would lead them out of the desert

> to a land of freedom and peace,
> a land where milk and honey flowed,
> As that promise is fulfilled again this night
> may they taste and see
> the goodness of your endless love.

At communion, after sharing in the Bread and Cup, the neophytes could be presented by the cate-chist with a cup of the blessed honey and milk with a few suitable words.

The panorama of Christian life can be seen if the Memento for the dead concludes the Eucharistic Prayer. Especially in this third Prayer with its extended commemoration of the dead, the end of Christian life for which Baptism is the beginning is clearly portrayed.

Easter Day

The Vigil is the true Easter service, but not every-one can attend. How then to create something spe-cial for the day's liturgies that is true to the great symbols of light and darkness, death and rebirth, womb and tomb? The sacramentary calls for a re-newal of baptismal promises and a communal sprin-kling. Infant Baptisms are also appropriate (espe-cially by immersion) and work better than at the night vigil.

The light requires more imagination. Obviously it is impossible to act as if it were night or as if the Candle were being lit for the first time. It is easy, though, to transform the penitential rite into an acclamation of praise for the light of the risen Lord.

The ritual is simple. The entrance procession does not end at the usual place but at a gathering around the Candle. After the usual greeting and call to worship, the presider speaks the acclamations that lead into the singing of the "Christ our Light! Thanks be to God!" dialogue.

An additional advantage of this adaptation is that the same procedure can be repeated with different acclamations on some of the Sundays of Easter. This is a simple but effective way to keep the Candle and its meaning alive in the prayer of the community. The Candle can also be incensed during each portion of the dialogue as a gesture of reverence and praise.

OPENING LIGHT SERVICE

When everything is prepared, the procession of acolytes, readers, and concelebrants enters by the usual route. They gather, though, around the Easter Candle, forming a large circle with the concelebrants facing the community. The PC then begins the service.

The Greeting

PC: In the name of the Father +, and of the Son, and of the Holy Spirit.

ALL: Amen.

PC: May the peace of the risen Lord be with you!

ALL: And also with you!

As a call to worship, the PC gives an explanation of the symbol of the Candle and its flame. He then invites everyone to pray.

The Acclamations

The acclamations may be proclaimed by an ACC, the PC, or a cantor.

Standing in front of the Candle, an acolyte may incense the Candle during each singing of "Christ our Light!"

ACC/PC/CANTOR: Lord Jesus, you have conquered the darkness of our ignorance and selfishness, of our loneliness and discouragement and pain....Filled with your light, we sing: Christ our light!

ALL: Thanks be to God!

ACC/PC/CANTOR: Lord Jesus, you have overcome the darkness of our hatred and indifference, of oppression and discrimination....Filled with your love, we sing: Christ our light!

ALL: Thanks be to God!

ACC/PC/CANTOR: Lord Jesus, we have so often chosen darkness, but your glory has filled our hearts and minds and bodies....Christ our light!

ALL: Thanks be to God!

The Gloria may be begun immediately.

The Opening Prayer

Everyone has his or her own personal moment that is hallowed by emotion and memory. For me the whole celebration of Holy Week and the Triduum is summed up in the Easter Invitation to Communion, which has become a tradition in my parish:

PC: This is the Lamb of God, slain yet triumphant, who takes away the sin of the world. This is the Body and Blood of our risen Lord who is among us now and till the end of time. This is the gift of the Spirit for eternity. Happy are we who are called to the wedding feast of the Lamb! Alleluia!

Removing
Baptismal Garments

One part of Easter mystagogy that was not restored in the RCIA is the laying aside of the baptismal garments at the end of Easter Octave. This gesture was so vivid in the ancient world that it gave one of the names for the Second Sunday of Easter: *post albas (deponendas),* after (laying aside) the white robes.

Reviving this gesture could seem a bit antiquarian (a rite for taking off clothes in church!), but the lack of special ritual during mystagogia is a problem. Perhaps there is the hint of something here to build upon. The following rite is an attempt to develop the ancient ritual into a rite of passage. The first phase in the neophytes' life in the Church is ended by the gesture of disrobing; the second is begun by their welcome to the body of the faithful in the Exchange of Peace.

The texts with the disrobing evoke the experiences that they shared just eight days before—the crucial element in early mystagogia. The Exchange of Peace also repeats a gesture from the Easter Vigil, but the accompanying prayer based upon the day's gospel of Doubting Thomas hopefully adds a new dimension to the experience.

This celebration would also be an appropriate occasion to include within the homily a witness talk by one or two of the newly initiated about what they have experienced through the RCIA process.

A RITE FOR
REMOVING THE WHITE GARMENTS
AND WELCOMING THE
NEWLY INITIATED ON EASTER (II)

The newly baptized (and those newly received if they too wore white robes for Easter Vigil) wear the robes for this Eucharist. They may also be part of the entrance procession.

This rite may be concelebrated by a presbyter or deacon or by two presbyters.

After the homily the concelebrants come to stand at the head of the main aisle facing the congregation.

ACC/PC: Would those who have just been initiated at Easter Vigil please come forward with their sponsors! (*He may call each by name.*)

The newly initiated come forward and stand facing the concelebrants with their sponsors behind them. A presbyter addresses them with these or similar words.

The Instruction and Disrobing

PC/ACC: (*to the newly baptized*)
Dear N.&N., here on Easter night
you were reborn by water and the Holy Spirit,
here in this font you became a new creation
and clothed yourself in Christ.

(*To the newly received*)
Dear N.&N., here on Easter night

you professed the fullness of the Christian faith
and (with the newly baptized) were sealed
with the gift of the Holy Spirit.
Together you were nourished
by the Body and Blood
of our risen Lord.

(*To all the newly initiated*)
And so for eight days
(some of) you have worn a white garment
to proclaim
that you truly are God's beloved
son(s) and daughter(s).
But today it is time
to lay aside these outward signs
and to take your place
with your older brothers and sisters
in this Church.

Always remember the love that led you here,
and keep your hearts faithful and untainted by sin.
When at last like the disciples of old
we see our risen Lord face to face,
he will call us his friends
and welcome us into everlasting life.

ACC/PC: Would the sponsors please help the newly initiated remove their white garments.

*The acolytes take the white garments form the
sponsors and remove them to the side.*

The General Intercession and Exchange of Peace

PC/ACC: Let us stand and pray!

The reader or cantor comes to the lectern to begin the General Intercessions, with the musicians introducing the response in the usual way.
A presbyter concludes the Intercessions with the following prayer:

PC/ACC:
Lord Jesus Christ, on the day of your resurrection,
you appeared to the fearful
and wished them: Peace!
You breathed on them
and gave them the Holy Spirit.
Today you revealed yourself again to the doubting
and revealed the fullness of your love.

Reveal yourself now
to N.&N./these new members of your Church,
Strengthen their faith; purify their love;
fill them anew with the Spirit of forgiveness.
At every moment may they live by your grace.
And fill all of us here with your peace,
that peace which this world cannot give.
Make us true members of your Body,
filled with the peace and unity of that kingdom
where you live and reign in glory forever and ever.

ALL: Amen!

PC/ACC: May the peace of the risen Lord be always with you!

ALL: And also with you!

ACC/PC: Let us now greet N.&N. and each other, sharing our common bond in the peace of Christ,
The exchange of peace is a bit more extended than usual. When the exchange is finished, a concelebrant addresses the community in these or similar words:

The Instruction Before the Eucharist

ACC/PC: As one family let us feast again at the banquet of our risen Lord.

The newly initiated immediately go to make the presentation of the gifts.

Pentecost

Many of the ideas treated here were also explored in "Pentecost: the Fiftieth Day," Liturgy 3, no. 1 (Winter 1982.)

Red. Tongues of flame. Fire of love. Bright vestments and June roses. The kaleidoscope of images and memories that Pentecost evokes has a quality different from any other liturgical celebration. Perhaps because no other celebration has a color as its central icon. Christmas calls forth the manger scene; Easter, the draped cross or the towering candle; Pentecost—red.

Or perhaps it is different because it is the end that is also the beginning. In Roman Catholic parishes, the RCIA team is at last finished with another group of new Roman Catholics. In many churches, a new group of teenagers is confirmed. The worship committee doesn't have to worry again till the fall. The school year is ending with a commencement. All around the pace of summer is beginning.

Whatever the reason, Pentecost has a unique quality. The lectionary for the day Eucharist reinforces that quality. The reading from Acts follows the Lucan chronology and places the giving of the Spirit on the fiftieth day after the Resurrection, in rushing wind and parted flame. The gospel is Johannine and depicts Jesus quietly breathing the Spirit upon the church on Easter Day itself. And, beside all the images of fire, the day epistle and the vigil gospel urge us to "drink deep" of the "flowing water." For those in the community who are not poets, this rich panorama of images must be confusing.

How are we to celebrate such a festival? What gestures, objects, and words can act out such richness? The two scriptural chronologies are only superficially incoherent. In both, the risen Christ is entrusting his friends with a new mission: to reconcile humankind with God. In both, his last gift is the Spirit, who empowers them for this ministry. Easter emphasizes the beginning of this process in the glorification of Jesus; Pentecost, its continuation in the church.

What should we do then? We should continue our celebration of Easter. The Candle still burns in our midst, but the flowers and ribbons that decorate it can be of a different color. The alleluias should still be those we have sung for the forty-nine days before, but there is music that is more pentecostal. There are the old favorites, but some newer music more clearly integrates Easter and Pentecost, for example, "We Know that Christ is Raised and Dies No More." The following Kyrie tropes can enhance the entrance rite. The dismissal should also include the Easter alleluias.

PENTECOST KYRIE TROPES

Cantor
Lord Je - sus Christ You have con - quered death and filled us with Your life; Ky -

Congregation   Cantor
r - i - e e - le - i - son. Ky - r - i - e e - le - i - son. Lord

Je - sus Christ You have as - cen - ded to God's right hand for - e - ver

Congregation
plead- ing for us: Christe e - le - i - son Christe

Cantor
e - le - i - son Lord Je - sus Christ, You fill us with Your spir - it and

send us forth to pro - claim that You are Lord: Ky - r - i - e e -

Congregation
le - i - son Ky - r - i - e e - le - i - son.

Simple gestures can also be effective. As in some other celebrations, we should invite the whole community to move out of the pews and join hands across the aisles for the Lord's Prayer. This powerfully evokes the unity amid diversity within the living Body of Christ. The invitation to peace that follows can be built upon the day gospel, wherein the gift of the Spirit is linked with the Lord's peace.

The most appropriate ritual for the celebration is a renewal of baptismal promises by the community as is done on Easter Day. In the following rite, the invitation has been composed as an attempt to integrate Easter and Pentecost as parts of one festival. The promises are based upon the version given in the Roman Catholic Rite of Confirmation. They have been adapted both by including more images and by involving references to the whole church. (The Roman liturgical books so often state that the Spirit descended upon the apostles at Pentecost; the Acts of the Apostles says "the whole community of believers.") The blessing of the water is adapted from the Easter Vigil.

To avoid overloading the rite with too many presider's words, a communal acclamation can be introduced into the blessing. Some of the brief acclamations suggested for the Eucharistic Prayers for Children would work. The Rite of Baptism for Children (RBC 223-4) suggests a similar adaptation for that service. From my experience, having the musicians play quietly behind the presider's proclamation both unifies the total verbal/aural event and makes the lead-in for the community acclamation much more smooth.

Another playful touch can be added with the sprinkling. We should not be afraid to be generous in this gesture. A bowl easy enough for an adult to carry, yet filled with water, is needed. Two or three 10-inch-long evergreen branches bound together with florist's tape will provide an experience of rain from above if the presider has a good arm and aims a bit overhead. At Easter we usually bind some forsythia in with the branches; on Pentecost, we use some roses or any other red flower that is in bloom.

We must not downplay such touches: in liturgy the symbolic *is* the real. A friend recently shared with me an experience of why Pentecost means so much to her. Four years ago she had been caught up in the service and was enjoying singing along during the sprinkling when suddenly from behind her came a splatter of water over her head and a red petal landed upon her hymnal, and she said: This is real! Her sense of God's presence in her life is still affected by the power of that moment.

This feast is also one of the Sundays most suitable for Infant Baptism. The usual baptismal sequence can be adapted by substituting some of the proper texts in the accompanying rite as alternatives.

SEQUENCE WITH INFANT BAPTISM

The letters (A), (B) and (B alternate), (C), and (D) indicate the appropriate substitutions from the sprinkling rite.

1. The Blessing of Water (B alternate)
2. The Instruction to Parents
3. The Baptismal Promises (A)
4. The Baptism
5. The Explanatory Rites
   Chrismation
   Clothing with White Garment
   Presentation of Lighted Candle
6. The Sprinkling (C)
7. The Instruction before the Eucharist (D)

If adults are to be initiated on Pentecost, similar textual alterations could be made.

SEQUENCE OF
ADULT BAPTISM/PROFESSION OF
FAITH AND CONFIRMATION

The letters (A), (B) and (B alternate), (C), and (D) indicate the appropriate substitutions from the sprinkling rite.

1. The Blessing of Water
   with Baptism (B alternate)
   with only Profession (B)
2. The Instruction to Candidates
3. The Promises (A)
4. The Reception into Full Communion
5. The Baptism
6. The Explanatory Rites
   White Garment
   Presentation of the Candle
7. The Confirmation
8. The Sprinkling (C)
9. The Instruction before the Eucharist (D)

RENEWAL OF BAPTISMAL PROMISES ON PENTECOST

The sprinkling bowl and branch are prepared beforehand on a small table to the right of the sanctuary. The rite is conducted from beside the table.

Facing the community, one of the concelebrants asks all to stand. A presbyter then leads this rite.

The Invitation

PC/ACC: My brothers and sisters, on Easter night we were all baptized again into the saving death and resurrection of Christ, and renewed that covenant of love which binds us to God and to one another.

Now our fifty days of celebration are completed, for today we celebrate how Jesus completely fulfilled his Easter promise of new life in the Spirit.

If you are willing to commit yourself anew to God and to each other in the church, I ask you to respond: Yes, I do believe! to each of the following questions.

The Promises (A)

PC/ACC: Do you believe in God, the almighty Father and master of our destiny, who guides all creation by his Spirit?

ALL: Yes, I do believe!

172

PC/ACC: Do you believe in Jesus Christ God's Son, conceived by the Spirit, anointed by him at his Baptism, who was crucified, died, was buried, rose, and is now seated at the right hand of the Father to fill all creation with his blessings?

ALL: Yes, I do believe!

PC/ACC: Do you believe in the Holy Spirit, the Lord and Giver of life, who came to the apostles and the whole church at Pentecost, and who has come to us in Baptism and Confirmation?

ALL: Yes, I do believe!

PC/ACC: Do you believe in the Spirit's power to make us the one, holy, catholic church, the true Body of Christ, through the forgiveness of sins, the resurrection of the body, and the promise of life everlasting?

ALL: Yes, I do believe!

The presider extends his right hand over the bowl. An acclamation of praise may be sung at the points indicated.

The Blessing of Water (B)

ALL: (Acclamation.)

PC/ACC: Father, through many signs you reveal to us the wonders of your love.

At the dawn of creation, your Spirit breathed on the waters, making them the source of life and holiness.

In the fullness of time, your Son willed that blood and water should flow from his side as he hung on the cross so that all humankind might drink deep of his Spirit.

ALL: (Acclamation.)

PC/ACC: After his resurrection, he told his disciples: Go out and teach all nations, baptizing them in the name of the Father, the Son, and the Holy Spirit.

And so we ask you, Father, send your Holy Spirit upon this water +, which we shall use to recall our rebirth by water and the Spirit.

ALL: (Acclamation.)

PC/ACC: May all who have shared Christ's death in Baptism rise also with him to newness of life.

May the joy that has filled our hearts this Eastertime be fulfilled one day in the glory of heaven.

ALL: (Acclamation.)

PC/ACC: We ask this through Jesus, our risen Lord, by the power of the Spirit moving us to pray.

Praise and honor and glory be yours now and forever and ever!

ALL: (sing) Amen! Amen! Amen!

The Sprinkling (C)

PC/ACC: God has truly given us new birth by water and the Holy Spirit. Let us relive the water through which we came to our new life.

An acolyte carries the bowl, and the presider walks around the whole church sprinkling the community while everyone sings "Come, Holy Ghost" or another appropriate hymn.
When the sprinkling and singing are finished, the presider at the presbyters' bench addresses the community.

Instruction before the Eucharist (D)

PC/ACC: Dear friends, we have relived God's call and our adoption as his beloved sons and daughters in the church. Upon each of us some gift of the Spirit has come.

Now, as one united body, let us prepare to celebrate our Eucharist.

The Preparation of the Altar and Gifts begins immediately.

THE BLESSING OF WATER FOR BAPTISM (B alternate)

The Invitation

After the homily a presbyter or deacon goes to stand by the font and faces the congregation.

PC/ACC:
My dear brothers and sisters,
let us now ask God to bless this water
and to give N&N/these children/the elect
new life in the Spirit. Let us stand and pray.

After a pause, the PC/ACC extends his or her hand over the font and the musicians begin the acclamation.

The Blessing

ALL: (Acclamation)

PC/ACC:
Father, through many signs
you reveal to us the wonders of your love.
At the dawn of creation,
your Spirit breathed on the waters,
making them the source of life and holiness.
In the fullness of time,
your Son willed that blood and water
should flow from his side as he hung on the cross
so that all humankind
might drink deep of his Spirit.

ALL: (Acclamation)

PC/ACC:
After his resurrection,
he told his disciples: Go out and teach all nations,
baptizing them in the name of the Father,
the Son, and the Holy Spirit.
And so we ask you, Father,
send your Holy Spirit
upon the water of this font +.

ALL: (Acclamation)

PC/ACC:
May all who share here in Christ's death
through Baptism
rise also with him to newness of life.
May all who are sprinkled with this water
share anew in the gift of the Spirit.
May the joy that has filled our hearts
this Eastertime
be fulfilled one day in the glory of heaven.

ALL: (Acclamation)

PC/ACC:
We ask this through Jesus, our risen Lord,
by the power of the Spirit moving us to pray.
Praise and honor and glory be yours
now and forever and ever!

ALL: (sing) Amen! Amen! Amen!

PART TWO:
Rites of Initiation for Roman Catholic Children

Infant Baptism

As Christ was anointed
Priest, Prophet, and King,
so may you always live
as a member of his Body,
sharing everlasting life (RBC 62).

Good liturgy can be enjoyable, challenging, and—in its own way—seductive. If we grow accustomed to a vital sense of community, to good music, tasteful environment, and moving ritual, the personal level of expectation rises. Why don't all our services reach this level of involvement and celebration?

Trying to turn the Thirty-first Sunday in Ordinary Time into a "special" event, and the Thirty-second, and the Thirty-third, leads straight to burnout. Yet the level of celebration we attain for festivals should be the inspiration and the criterion that keep us from allowing the ordinary to become the shoddy or perfunctory. If nothing else, our memories of ritual done more richly help us appreciate the simpler gestures of Ordinary Time.

One clear example of this process is my experience of the symbols and rituals of initiation at Easter Vigil. Hearing adults publicly profess their belief, seeing and hearing the water flow over them, seeing and smelling the Holy Chrism, the white garments, the burning candles—all the sensory stimuli that surround rebirth as God's sons and daughters have fixed the event and its joy firmly in my memory. Any theological explanation I can give of what Christian initiation means is founded upon those memories. I have seen and heard and smelled the action of the Spirit.

Yet Easter Vigil happens only once a year. What about our use of the same symbols and rituals in Infant Baptism? I have never forgotten the first time twenty years ago that I became a godparent. I remember fifteen minutes of words punctuated by dab, dribble, dab as the two anointings and actual Baptism occurred, followed by the presentation of a white handkerchief that was immediately retrieved. This event remains for me the worst-case scenario, but I suspect that in many parishes the situation has not drastically altered. For good reasons and bad, a minimalist and legalistic approach to Infant Baptism keeps this sacramental celebration from achieving its potential within the spiritual life of American Catholics. Yet we know it can be better.

About twelve years ago, my parish's worship commission and parish council re-examined our overall baptismal practice. Several reasons prompted our reappraisal. We were just beginning adult RCIA, and a large number of children were being born. Moreover, as a university parish, we were encountering an unusual situation. A large proportion of the infants being baptized in the church were not the children of parishioners but of alumni/ae who were asking their favorite Jesuit teacher to perform the ceremony for their children. What were our various responsibilities? How could we make sense out of potential discord?

After several months of discussion, writing, and revision, we finally adopted a Statement of Belief and Policy, which, with minor revisions, has remained in force ever since. Its general principles are few. First, any Baptism brings forgiveness of sin, adoption as God's daughter or son, and entrance into the community. Second, the same three elements are part of Infant Baptism. A healing of flawed human nature takes place as Baptism begins the infant's years of growth in Christ under the guidance of both family and community. Infant Baptism (like First Communion) is not just a private event. The infant is born into a family; by Baptism he or she is reborn into the entire community of believers (cf., RBC 4).

These few principles have given clear guidance for concrete policies. First, adults are baptized or received only at Easter Vigil. Second, infants are normally baptized at parish Sunday Eucharists at fixed intervals throughout the year. Third, only children of registered parishioners are baptized in the parish. Other children should be baptized where their growth will take place. Fourth, parents are expected to participate in a brief preparation program. Fifth, priests and deacons who are relatives or friends are welcome to concelebrate and participate in the baptismal ritual, but a priest associated with the parish will preside. Lastly, exceptions are made for pastoral reasons by the parish staff.

Though not everyone was pleased that the free-wheeling days were over, this Statement has provided our community with a coherent framework within which both the educational program and the liturgical celebration have had a chance to grow. Having stated our beliefs and committed ourselves to their concrete embodiment, we began working together at the task. The experience has been sometimes painful but ultimately rewarding for the whole parish.

The current working of the program reflects the advantage of being a small parish of 450 registered households. We can get by with six Baptism Sundays a year at approximately two-month intervals. These are carefully synchronized with the major liturgical seasons. The midwinter celebration is always scheduled for the Baptism of the Lord, for example. There are none during Lent but rather on Easter Day or the following Sunday. In Ordinary Time any Sunday is basically appropriate. (I have heard some good homilies in which the awareness of Baptism added a whole new perspective to the lectionary selections.) What is crucial is that the dates be announced for the whole year in advance. In mobile America people need a great deal of lead-time to bring their families together.

On a Baptism Sunday the sacrament is celebrated at every Eucharist if people who regularly attend a given service have an infant to be baptized. In August, 9 a.m. might have one; 11 a.m., three; and 7:30 p.m., two. In November, 9 a.m. might have two; 11

a.m., zero; and 7:30 p.m., three. Wherever people find their primary community, they celebrate the sacrament; there is no need to isolate the celebration into one service. Hopefully there will be no more than four at a given service. Above that number logistics and time considerations become complicated.

The preparation program has evolved into an experience of building community. When the new parents contact the parish staff, the director of religious education (DRE) does a preliminary screening of their level of faith commitment and involvement before working out with them the probable dates for the preparatory meeting and the actual Baptism. Short materials from various publishers about choosing sponsors and the meaning of Baptism are provided.

The preparatory meeting is chaired by two to four individuals out of a pool of six couples who have been prepared by extra study, reflection, and training. The meeting begins by a sharing of personal histories and moves into faith-sharing and a discussion of what understanding and hopes the parents have for their child from this event. A short movie, *Godparent Gussie,* is shown and discussed.

After a break there is a homemade slideshow on the different symbols and gestures in the rite. This provides a chance for further sharing and reflection as well as alerting people to practical matters. Why should immersion be considered the "normal" mode of Baptism? What is the difference between the two anointings? Why bother to dress the infant *during* the service? How does one decorate a baptismal candle? By raising and discussing such questions in the preparatory meeting, the actual rehearsal one or two weeks later will run smoothly.

Even parents who have been through the program before are asked to participate, and most do. Their contribution to the discussion and sharing is both inspirational and informative for the first-timers. Through the sharing of stories and memories, concrete community is formed, new dreams are dreamt, and traditions established.

Adapting the actual rite requires fidelity to the tradition, a sense of ritual and community involvement, and much trial-and-error. The post-Vatican II rite of Baptism for children is clearly based on the adult RCIA but combines catechumenal and initiation rites into one continuous service. The rite outside of Eucharist presumes a great deal of movement: reception at the door, procession to the place where the Liturgy of the Word is celebrated, procession (if necessary) to the font, procession to the altar for the Lord's Prayer and blessing—even though in practice few clergy seem to take these movements seriously. The rite within Eucharist (a completely new post-Vatican II creation) involves less movement, but the number of words and gestures remains the same.

And there lies the great difficulty we have experienced with the current rite. Almost nothing is dropped from the Eucharist, but a great deal is added. The additions also have catechumenal and initiatory rites of primary, secondary, and little importance all running on so that what is crucial has no chance to be experienced as such. The community has real difficulty figuring out what is going on, much less being prayerfully involved. The only solution would be to reorganize the elements into a more coherent dramatic structure (cf., RBC 28, where such a rearrangement is suggested when infants are baptized at Easter Vigil).

THE PRELIMINARY SERVICE

This service takes place in a side chapel.

1. The Greeting (Order of Mass)
2. Reception of the Child
   questions of commitment (RBC 37-40)
   signing with the cross (RBC 41)
3. Litany of the Saints (RBC 48)
4. Prayer of Exorcism (RBC 49)
5. Anointing with the Oil of Catechumens (RBC 50)
6. Dismissal (RBC 70D)

Taking a cue from the adult RCIA, we could arrange in a side chapel a semi-public service scheduled fifteen minutes before Eucharist. All the family and friends would be invited into more intimate surroundings, where all the rites before the water blessing would be celebrated. A real sense of family solidarity would be built as everyone heard the parents and godparents make their commitment to the infants' Christian development and as everyone signed the little ones with the cross. The invocation of the saints evokes memories of others who have borne those names before: grandparents, siblings, etc. The anointing with the Oil of Catechumens as an exorcism becomes much clearer when separated from the chrismation. In short, without depriving the total community of any gesture or symbol of primary importance, these preliminary rites could speak most strongly in more intimate surroundings.

The parents, godparents, and infants would then wait in the small chapel for the processional to begin, while the other family members and friends go immediately to join the congregation.

After the procession and greeting, the penitential rite would be omitted as is the general practice in the Roman Rite when another liturgical service precedes the Eucharist (cf., Liturgy of the Hours 93-94.) Instead the principal concelebrant briefly introduces the parents and children and then proclaims the Opening Prayer. The Liturgy of the Word would follow the usual pattern until after the homily. The General Intercessions would be omitted because they are redundant of other prayers. The remaining elements of the Infant Baptism ritual would then be celebrated.

INFANT BAPTISM

One through four take place at the font.

1. Blessing of Water and Chrism (RBC 54 and 223-224)
2. Baptismal Promises (RBC 56-59 and RCIA 351)
3. Baptism (RBC 60)
4. Chrismation (RBC 61)

Five through seven take place at the head of the main aisle:

5. Song during the Dressing
6. White Garment (RBC 63)
7. Presentation of the Lighted Candle (RBC 64)

The concelebrating priest who is to lead the blessing should simply go stand beside the font, facing the congregation. Except at Easter Vigil, we should not use the blessing in the form given at RBC 54. Though a moving summary of the events of salvation history, it is not written for communal participation and needs more musical talent than most clergy possess.

The RBC provides two alternatives at 223 and 224. Arranged in a litanic pattern, they presume congregational participation and allow the concelebrant to speak the invocations over a musical background that leads the community into the refrain. By such simple enhancement, this solemn blessing can become a climactic moment of praise and intercessions within the rite.

These alternatives could be further adapted. RBC 223 is lengthy and involves switching refrains in the middle. The following text is an attempt to resolve these difficulties by combining the six invocations into three, all addressed to the First Person of the Trinity.

THE BLESSING AND INVOCATION OF GOD OVER THE WATER AND CHRISM (A)

The Invitation

PRESBYTER or DEACON: *(standing by the font)*
My dear brothers and sisters, let us now ask God to give these children new life in abundance through this water and his Holy Spirit.
Let us kneel in prayer.

After a pause, the cantor sings the chosen refrain only once. The presbyter or deacon stands and proclaims the following invocations with the refrain being repeated between each.

The Invocations

ALL: (Acclamation)

PRESBYTER or DEACON:
Praise to you, almighty God and Father,
for you have created water to cleanse and give life.
May all baptized here be washed clean of sin
and be born again as your children.

ALL: (Acclamation)

PRESBYTER or DEACON:
Praise to you, loving God,
for sending your only Son to die on the Cross,

that in the blood and water flowing from his side
and through his death and resurrection
the Church might be born.
May all those baptized here
be changed more and more perfectly
into his image.

ALL: (Acclamation)

PRESBYTER or DEACON:
Praise to you, faithful God,
for sending the Holy Spirit to anoint your Messiah
at his Baptism in the waters of the Jordan.
Send him now to make this water holy +.
May all whom you have chosen in our day
be born again by the Spirit's power.

ALL: (Acclamation)

PRESBYTER or DEACON:
This chrism also, Father, you have made holy
through the prayer of our bishop N.
May those anointed with it today
be consecrated by the Holy Spirit
and take their place among your holy, your royal,
your priestly and prophetic people.

ALL: (Acclamation)

The Prayer

*After the singing of the final refrain, the presbyter
or deacon says:*

PRESBYTER or DEACON: Father, you have called your children (N./N./N.) to this font that they might share in the faith of your Church and have eternal life.

By the mystery of this consecrated water and chrism, lead them to a new, a spiritual birth in Christ Jesus.

Through him we give you thanks and praise,
by the power of the Holy Spirit,
now and forever and ever.

ALL: (sing) Amen.

RBC 224 could also be adapted by changing the acclamations into invocations.

THE BLESSING AND INVOCATION OF GOD OVER THE WATER AND CHRISM (B)

The Invitation

PRESBYTER or DEACON: *(standing by the font)*
My dear brothers and sisters, let us now ask God to give these children new life in abundance through this water and his Holy Spirit.
Let us kneel in prayer.

After a pause, the cantor proclaims the chosen refrain only once. The presbyter or deacon stands and proclaims the following invocations with the refrain being repeated between each.

The Invocations

ALL: (Acclamation)

PRESBYTER or DEACON:
Father, God of mercy,
bless this water +,
and fill with new life
those who shall be baptized in it
as your very own children.

ALL: (Acclamation)

PRESBYTER or DEACON:
Loving God,
bless this water +,
and make all those baptized
by water and the Holy Spirit
into one people, united in your Son Jesus.

ALL: (Acclamation)

PRESBYTER or DEACON:
Faithful God,
bless this water +;
set those baptized in it truly free.
Fill them with the Spirit of your love,
that they may live in your peace.

ALL: (Acclamation)

PRESBYTER or DEACON:
Father, you have made this chrism holy
by the prayer of our bishop N.
May those anointed with it today
proclaim the Good News of Jesus everywhere.

ALL: (Acclamation)

The Prayer
After the last refrain, the presbyter or deacon says:)

PRESBYTER or DEACON: Father, you have called your children N./N./N. to this font that they might share in the faith of your Church and have eternal life.

By the mystery of this consecrated water and chrism, lead them to a new, a spiritual birth in Christ Jesus. Through him we give you thanks and praise, by the power of the Holy Spirit, now and forever and ever.

ALL: (sing) Amen.

The pattern can be easily imitated. The following composition is a contemporary attempt at this format.

THE BLESSING AND INVOCATION OF GOD OVER THE WATER AND CHRISM (C)

PRESBYTER or DEACON (*standing by the font*):
My dear brothers and sisters, let us now ask God to give these children new life in abundance through this water and his Holy Spirit.
Let us kneel in prayer.

After a pause, the cantor proclaims the chosen refrain only once. The presbyter or deacon stands and proclaims the following invocations with the refrain being repeated between each.

The Invocations

ALL: (Acclamation)

PRESBYTER or DEACON:
We thank you, eternal God, for rushing streams,
for placid lakes and mighty ocean,
for thunderstorms in summer's heat,
for gentle rain that makes the seed to grow
and earth to blossom.
Bless this water +: make it for us today
the source of life.

ALL: (Acclamation)

PRESBYTER or DEACON:
We thank you, faithful God,
for deliverance from the Flood,

for liberation at the Red Sea,
for refreshment amid the rocky desert,
for the prophets' promise of a new covenant
of overflowing love.
Bless this water +: make it for us today
the sign of your presence.

ALL: (Acclamation)

PRESBYTER or DEACON:
We thank you, loving God, for Jesus:
for his Baptism in the Jordan,
for the river of life that flowed
from his side on the cross,
for his resurrection and his Spirit
leaping up within us as a living fountain.
Bless this water +: make it for us today
the source of rebirth.

ALL: (Acclamation)

PRESBYTER or DEACON:
We thank you, Father, for Jesus:
for his anointing as your Son at the Jordan,
for his anointing there as your Servant,
for the Spirit who comes to rest
upon all the baptized.
May those marked today with this Holy Chrism
be consecrated as your own.

ALL: (Acclamation)

The Prayer

After the final refrain, the presbyter or deacon says:

PRESBYTER or DEACON: Father, you have called your children N./N./N. to this font that they might share in the faith of your Church and have eternal life.

By the mystery of this consecrated water and chrism, lead them to a new, a spiritual birth in Christ Jesus. Through him we give you thanks and praise, by the power of the Holy Spirit, now and forever and ever.

ALL: (sing either once or three times)
Amen!

One consistent element in these adaptations is the inclusion of a reference to the Holy Chrism. Most Catholics are ignorant of the rich tradition connected with this perfumed oil, or associate it solely with ordination. Yet the consecration prayers for the chrism (other than a passing reference in the alternate text to "every place and thing signed with this holy oil") speak only of its use in the initiation rites. All the baptized are described there as the Lord's Anointed, as the consecrated priests, prophets, and kings of the new covenant.

The widespread practice of using a truly fragrant oil restores much of the symbol's unique significance, as does application of a sufficiently generous amount that much of the assembly can actually smell the chrism. A brief verbal reference still seems needed to open up the meaning of the symbol for those who are not used to it.

Only after the concluding Amen to the water blessing should the parents, godparents, and infants gather at the font. Little ones are squiggly and cute, and the climax of the rite is theirs, but putting them centerstage only for the heart of the rite helps keep them from becoming uncomfortable and disruptive.

The instruction and promises that follow in the rite are ambiguous. As written, they are addressed solely to the parents and godparents, but the question immediately before each individual Baptism states that we have all just professed the faith together. If the communal aspect of this sacrament is going to be clear, then everyone must be asked to stand and join in the promises. The following revision is a proposal for dealing with that ambiguity (cf., RBC 93).

Invitation

PC/ACC:
Dear parents and godparents,
you have come here
to present these children for Baptism.
By water and the Holy Spirit,
they are to receive the gift of new life
from God, who is love.
On your part, you must make it your constant care
to bring them up in the practice of faith,
in the fullness of that divine life
which God lavishes on them today.
If you are ready to accept this responsibility,
renew now the vows of your own Baptism.
Reject sin; profess your faith in Christ Jesus.
And to support you in this task,
I invite all here present
to renew these promises with you.
Would everyone please stand.

An effective way of reinforcing that common profession would be to use the Nicene Creed rather than the question/answer format. There are enough clerical words in the rite; a strong recitation of a familiar text can create a real sense of energy as the cadence of the lines moves along. The text's original significance as a daily or weekly reminder of baptismal covenant might enter again into our common liturgical memory.

Our experience with the current rite has taught us not to group the families around the font but behind it, facing the congregation. Some visibility for everyone is thus a possibility; the musicians can see as well as hear when to lead the community in an alleluia refrain for each Baptism (cf., RBC 60), and movement to the side for the dressing becomes simpler. Seeing the naked child lowered three times into the font and smeared all over his or her head (cf., RBC 62) with about a teaspoon of the Holy Chrism is more important than any photograph or videotape of the event; this new event becomes the *living* icon for everyone present of their own Baptism. The singing especially restates with joy the community's involvement and commitment.

After the last child is baptized and chrismated, the ritual relaxes for a moment before the remaining explanatory rites. Dressing babies in outfits can be a little time consuming, and the concelebrants need to dry their hands and remove the excess oil. With larger numbers of infants being baptized, it is best for practicality's sake to have one concelebrant baptize and another chrismate (cf., RBC 62). Communal song praying for the children works most effectively during these moments. Carey Landry's "Song of Baptism" or Michael Joncas' "I Have Loved You" are good examples, and two stanzas are usually about right for the amount of time the dressing takes.

The parents, godparents, and infants are led back to the front of the sanctuary facing the congregation. A concelebrant says the formula for the white garment. He lights each baptismal candle from the big Easter Candle in the main aisle, says the presentation formula, and leads in a rousing round of applause. The parents leave the candles burning on the altar to show the connection between their child's Baptism and the Eucharist, and then sit down and relax because their special part in the service is finished.

The godparents make the presentation of the gifts. Within the Eucharistic Prayer, one of the mementos for newly baptized infants (cf., RCIA old 391, new 242) can also be used. The Lord's Prayer may also be introduced by some version of the long formula given at RBC 68. One of the four final final blessings at RBC 70 can conclude the service, or a seasonal final blessing might be more appropriate, for example, in Eastertime. Yet none of these extra words is really necessary. Sunday Eucharist is the weekly covenant meal for the baptized, and the Roman liturgy reflects that fact. Its ordinary texts can serve quite well for a celebration of Baptism.

There are two other lessons we have learned about such celebrations at Sunday Eucharist. First is the need for extra hospitality. Enough pews must be reserved for the infants' families and their friends. Ushers are a great help with this task, and also with making certain that strangers have all the participation aids they will need to join in the service. Provision for uncomfortable or disruptive children must also be made clear beforehand.

The second lesson is the need to make a polite but firm announcement just before the processional begins that no photographs or videotapes are permitted during the service. Good ritual and rich symbolism is photogenic but at the cost of destroying prayer, which is the point of the ritual. Nor are professionals necessarily less disruptive. I have unpleasant memories of one Infant Baptism where every gesture within the rite was momentarily halted so that the clergy, parents, and godparents could reposition themselves for the camerawoman. I was neither a witness to nor participant in the child's Baptism; instead I was part of a studio audience that witnessed the videotaping of the Baptism.

To generalize from a decade of experience, what makes a program of public Infant Baptism at Sunday Eucharist work? The answer lies in the same three elements that make RCIA or First Communion or any other special service work in the Sunday assembly.

First, the community is paramount. They and not the clergy or the family or whoever must *experience* that they are the primary liturgical actor in the service by word, song, and gesture. Their common prayer must not be disrupted but invited to open up and embrace these special people for this service.

Second, the service should be ordinary, that is, owned by the community in simple ways. There is no need to change the lectionary or hang banners or let the parents choose the music or recruit relatives as readers or distributors. Some parents want to turn the event into their show, but that is an abuse of the *common* worship. Letting the service *be* as the usual service for that Sunday works best.

Third, what is special should be special. Rehearsals so everyone is comfortable with the ritual are crucial. Real garments and real candles are important, as are lots of water and oil. Yet people are the most special. Letting the families' faith in God and love for their children be revealed in public is *the* essential ingredient if the service is to build up the communal life of prayer.

What effect has this program had upon the parish? Some try to avoid Baptism Sundays, but most seem to enjoy them. Since I sometimes like to eavesdrop at socials after Sunday Mass, I have noticed certain comments beginning to appear as parishioners offer congratulations to adolescent confirmandi or to first communicants. Quite ordinary people who are not relatives start by saying: "I remember when you were baptized" as they launch into a story. And so, slowly, maybe we really are becoming a family, God's family, baptized and anointed as Christ's Body, sharing generation by generation in his everlasting life.

Confirmation

Experiences with adults and the RCIA have provided a powerful stimulus for religious educators and for liturgists in this country. Even a brief perusal of the materials available for Confirmation or First Communion preparation reveals the marked impact the RCIA has had, especially in our awareness of process.

Yet adaptation does not mean point-for-point imitation. The kind of process that adults are going through in preparation for Easter Vigil differs in many important respects from the process through which Confirmation or First Communion candidates are passing. The RCIA is a model to be used, not abused.

The differences become especially apparent in the late winter and in spring when two and sometimes three sacramental preparation programs are occurring simultaneously. If nothing else, the difficulties in scheduling everything make certain decisions necessary. Recently, for example, our parish had four adults preparing for Easter Vigil, sixteen children preparing for First Communion two weeks later, and ten adolescents preparing for Confirmation two weeks after that, as well as another five

couples in the final phase of Infant Baptism preparation. Just trying to fit the minimum in meant that
we had some hard questions to ask and to try to
answer.

First, the worship life of the total community
seemed to us to be the ultimate concern. The desire
to celebrate and have a festival is a sign of health;
yet there is a parallel need for stability and for the
ordinary time of quiet growth in the Spirit. In a
small parish like ours, we learn quickly when people
are getting tired of something special going on every
Sunday.

There is also a need for coherence. The average
parishioner does not know the details of the different programs. Bouncing back and forth from
week to week between adults and children would be
liturgical schizophrenia, fragmenting instead of en-
hancing the community's worship.

Second, process is crucial; but we become aware of
how different the processes are. The RCIA members
and the community are in an "engagement" period.
Adults are involved in the long and often difficult
process of adjusting values, lifestyles, and deep-
seated identities into a new whole. The Lenten
period is thus appropriately named "purification
and enlightenment," and these liturgical celebrations seemed to demand priority in public Sunday
worship.

The Confirmation candidates, all between thir-
teen and sixteen years old, were already full members of the community by Baptism and Eucharist.
Though as adolescents they were already making
many of their own decisions, to say that they were
now affirming an adult or lifetime commitment

would be a pretense. They too might be exploring new forms of relationship; but their perspective, like their identity, was still very much that of their families. We needed to help them explore; we needed to celebrate with them the Seal of Baptism; but most of all, we had to respect their tentative though genuine faith commitment.

Consequently, on one of the Ordinary Sundays before Lent, they were all called up front and introduced, the catechists gave a brief testimonial, everyone applauded in welcome, and we stood up to pray the General Intercessions. There was no other public service until the actual celebration of Confirmation. Their process focused upon small group dynamics and spiritual companionship.

A RITE OF ACCEPTANCE FOR CONFIRMATION CANDIDATES

The candidates are seated with their families in the congregation. Their sponsors do not participate actively in this rite.

After the homily everyone remains seated, and the chief catechist comes to the lectern.

The Presentation

CATECHIST: (*to the community*)
Brothers and sisters,
by Baptism
we have all become members of the Church,
full members of the Body of Christ.
Week by week in our parish assembly here,
we grow in that life in Christ as we all share
in Word and Eucharist,
in our common prayer and praise.

If we look around,
we can become aware of how richly
the Spirit has blessed this community
with diverse gifts,
gifts that we must share with one another
and with the world.

Today it is my privilege
to present to you some young people
from our parish
who have begun the process of preparing
for the sacrament of Confirmation.

They have been asked to participate
in education evenings,
in a service project,
and a retreat.
They have been asked to share more fully
in the prayer life of our parish
and in our religious education program.
Then in (*month*) they will be ready
to reaffirm publicly
their baptismal profession of faith
and to be marked
in the midst of this parish assembly
with the Seal of their Baptism.

As we welcome them today,
I would ask each of us
to pray for them during the coming months.
What personal gift of the Spirit
can you or I share with them?

And so I would like to present to you
these young people.

*The catechist calls each one by name and gives
some brief biographical details while each is coming
forward. The young people stand on the step of the
sanctuary, facing the congregation.*

The Acceptance

The catechist returns to her or his place. The presbyter or deacon who is to lead this rite comes down to the center of the main aisle between the young people and the congregation and faces the young people. The congregation remains seated.)

PC/ACC: (*to the candidates*)
Dear N.&N., sisters and brothers,
if you really wish to commit yourselves
to this process of preparation,
I ask you to answer: Yes, I do promise!
to these questions.

ACC: Do you promise to cooperate willingly in this program of preparation for Confirmation?

CANDIDATES: Yes, I do promise!

ACC: Do you promise to follow the guidance of the Spirit wherever it may lead you?

CANDIDATES: Yes, I do promise!

ACC: Do you promise to share your gifts of the Spirit with this community and the whole human family?

CANDIDATES: Yes, I do promise!

The congregation remains seated. The PC/ACC now turns to them and asks them the following questions.

PC/ACC:
If you, the members of this parish,
are willing to support these young people,
I ask you to respond: Yes, I do promise!
to these questions.
Do you promise to share in their preparation
by your prayers and encouragement?

ALL: Yes, I do promise!

ACC: Do you promise them your loving support and the good example of your Christian life?

ALL: Yes, I do promise!

Turning again to the candidates, the PC/ACC addresses them.

PC/ACC:
Dear N.&N., sisters and brothers,
in the name of the (*name of parish*) community,
I welcome each of you as a candidate
for the sacrament of Confirmation.
May God who has begun this good work in you
bring it to a successful completion.

(*to the community*)
Let us give them a sign of our acceptance and welcome!

The PC/ACC leads the community in applause. The candidates then return to their places. The General Intercessions begin immediately.

The actual celebration of the sacrament requires little comment except to call for authenticity in the ritual. The laying-on of hands does not have to be a generalized waving in the air but could be a genuine attempt to pray over each recipient. If the number of recipients is large, presbyters may assist the bishop in this imposition of hands. (cf., Confirmation 8, 9, 25.)

The community might also sing a simple refrain as a kind of mantra during this gesture.

Authenticity is destroyed if there is someone standing at the side of the sanctuary to wipe the Chrism off immediately. The message given by such a practice seems not so much hospitality as a fear that the Spirit might really come. If the oil is going to be used generously, then the candidates can be warned beforehand to have a handkerchief ready if they experience any difficulty.

A final observation: Most of our problems with both the theory and practice of this sacrament would be resolved if we rethought what we were doing in the light of our experiences with adults and the RCIA. History, theology, the liturgical books, and the new Code of Canon Law all presume that this sacrament belongs for Roman Catholic children between Baptism and First Communion, probably at age seven. Adopting that practice in this country would not only eliminate a certain schizophrenia among those who have to explain Confirmation one way to adult converts and another to Roman Catholic children but also open up new opportunities for creative religious education with adolescents.

First Communion:
Two Preliminary Services

with Rosemary G. Conrad

The process of revising our parish's celebration of First Communion is described fully in the next chapter. One of the crucial ideas that surfaced during those discussions was the need for a series of liturgical experiences to prepare the children for their full share in all the aspects of the communal Meal. Yet we felt those services should not imitate too closely adult RCIA rites for several reasons.

The children preparing for First Communion were in a process that was not so much explorative as developmental. Their faith was still firmly embedded in that of their families; what they were learning was a new way of participating in that common faith. (Purification as part of that process and how it relates to First Reconciliation is another question.) Liturgical experience is an important part of that growing process: they learn by *doing* and reflection and not just by instructions. As the *National Catholic Directory* 122 says,

> Children around the age of 7 tend to think concretely;
> they grasp concepts like "unity" and "belonging" from
> experiences, such as sharing, listening, eating, convers-
> ing, giving, thanking, and celebrating.

We decided to have no public service for them apart from the First Communion celebration itself. Instead, we would focus upon two semi-public services. We knew from the RCIA and from Infant Baptism how effective an intermediate-size group experience could be: the initiates see the realities of the larger community, yet there is still a chance for personal sharing. Gesture can be strong but intimate in such a setting.

And so within the religious education program, we set aside two evenings with a similar format. The first half of each evening was a liturgical service for children, parents, catechists, pastor, and some other members of the parish. The second portion was "class" for the children and a discussion period for the adults.

From a practical standpoint, such a format enabled us to get parents involved without adding another meeting to everyone's schedule. It also involved the parents in the preparation process in two significant ways. First, they experienced a kind of adult mystagogia in which their diverse understanding of the liturgical events could surface and be shared and in which various issues (such as dress) could be addressed and resolved. Second, they became involved in their child's catechesis. By sharing in the services and by reflecting on the event afterward with their child, they were participants in and not observers of what was happening. As the *National Catechetical Directory* 122 says:

Parents have a right and a duty to be intimately involved in preparing their children for First Communion. Catechesis aims to help the parents grow in understanding and appreciation of the Eucharist and participate readily in catechizing their children.

In creating the two actual services, we tried to make all the components intermediate and transitional. We gathered not in classroom or in church but in the small chapel. Dress was casual, but the pastor wore alb and stole. We arranged seating in a circle but stood and sat at appropriate moments. The introduction, readings, and songs followed the usual pattern of the liturgy, but we also showed the film *Bread and Wine*. There were formal gestures and words, but everyone got to act out each ritual.

What have we learned from doing these semi-public services? First, we saw that little things are important. The children selected the readings and songs and dialogued during the "homily." Yet they also helped set the circle up. They helped cut up the fruit, pour the cups, and clean up afterwards. Involvement and service were not words but actions modeled and shared in.

Second, children have questions. By taking familiar objects, actions, and words out of the sanctuary and into their midst, all sorts of comments and questions spontaneously arose both during class discussions and at home.

Third, parents have questions too. More intimate ritual evoked their rich heritage of sacramental life, of what coming to the Lord's table meant—or sometimes did not mean—to them. Discussion of practical issues simply evolved into adult religious education. We have found Carol Luebering's *Your Child's*

First Communion: A Look at Your Dreams an invaluable tool to use with parents at this stage of the preparation process.

Fourth, parents do become catechists. The second-grade teacher reports the noticeable difference between children whose parents have participated in the services and those whose have not, even in such simple tasks as getting their religious education homework done.

Yet the process deepens. One of the First Communion candidates this year lost a grandfather in February. The boy asked his parents if he could receive communion at the funeral. Since their responsibility to decide about their child's readiness had been told to them and acted out with them, the parents were comfortable with making such a choice. And so, after a little more discussion with his parents about what the Eucharist meant (and had meant to his grandfather), Michael first shared at the Lord's Table with the rest of his family during Grampa's funeral.

THE WORD OF GOD: A PREPARATORY RITE FOR FIRST COMMUNION

Everyone gathers informally in the small chapel or other chosen space. The processional cross and lectionary or Bible might be displayed. The presbyter or deacon leading the rite should vest with at least a stole.

The children are seated in a circle in the center of the group. The parents, sponsors, and others are seated in a larger circle around them. The PC is seated at the head of the circles.

Introductory Song

The catechist or a musician leads the assembly in a song of gathering and welcome.

The Greeting

PC: In the name of the Father +, and of the Son, and of the Holy Spirit.

ALL: Amen.

PC: The Lord be with you (*or another version from the Order of Mass*).

ALL: And also with you.

PC: (*says a few words of welcome, then*) Let us pray! (*Pause, followed by PC's spontaneous prayer*)

ALL: Amen.

The Word of God

Readings
> One or more from scripture, preferably by the children.

A song
> Either after one reading or between two.

A brief commentary
> By the catechist or the PC about the importance of God's Word in our lives as Christians.

The Signing with the Cross and the Lord's Prayer

PC: Tonight we are going to act out our prayer with gestures. I ask the children to stand and face the adults. I ask the adults to follow my lead in marking the children with the sign of the cross.

When everyone is ready, the PC leads the prayer with the following words:

Receive the sign of the cross on your ears +; may you hear the Word of God.
Receive the sign of the cross on your lips +; may you speak the Word of God loudly.
Receive the sign of the cross on your hands +; may you work at building God's kingdom.

Receive the sign of the cross on your heart +;
may the Word of God live in your heart by faith.

I would now ask the children to make the sign of
the cross on the hearts of the adults.

Receive the sign of the cross on your heart +;
may the Word of God live in your heart by faith.

Let us now all join our hands and say together the
prayer that our Brother Jesus has taught us.

ALL: Our Father...

The Blessing and Peace

*As soon as the Lord's Prayer is ended, the PC
raises his hand in blessing.*

PC: May God's peace be with each of us here;
and may the blessing of almighty God:
the Father +, the Son, and the Holy Spirit,
come upon you all and remain with you forever.

ALL: Amen.

PC: Let us share a sign of peace with each other.

A Common Meal:
A Preparatory Rite for First Communion

Everyone gathers informally in the small chapel or other chosen space. The lectionary or Bible might be displayed. Adults and children sit together in one large circle. In the center of the circle is a small table covered with an attractive cloth, possibly some flowers, and a candle or two. On the table are set a plate holding a small loaf of bread, another plate holding sections of fruit, a cup of cool water, and another cup of grape juice. The PC is seated at the head of the table.

Introductory Song

The catechist or a musician leads the assembly in a song of gathering and welcome.

The Greeting

PC: In the name of the Father +, and of the Son, and of the Holy Spirit.

ALL: Amen.

PC: The Lord be with you (*or another version from the Order of Mass*).

ALL: And also with you.

PC: (*says a few words of welcome, then*) Let us pray! (*Pause, followed by the PC's spontaneous prayer*)

ALL: Amen.

The Word of God

Readings
One or more from Scripture, preferably by the children.

A song
Either after one reading or between two

A brief commentary
By the catechist or the PC about the importance of common meals for the human family and about the Eucharist as the common meal of God's family

The Sharing of Food and Drink and the Lord's Prayer
Seated or standing by the table, the PC spreads wide his arms to pray.

PC:
Loving God,
by baptism we are all your children,
the brothers and sisters of Jesus.
We thank you tonight
for bringing us together
to share this food and drink.

May we always live in your friendship
and at peace with one another.
All praise to you, Father,
through Jesus our Savior,
in the power of the Holy Spirit.
Blessed be God forever!

ALL: Blessed be God forever!

The PC takes the plate of bread, holds it up while saying the following blessing, and then eats a portion himself, and hands the plate to the person beside him.

PC:
Blessed are you,
Lord our God, Creator of the whole world:
you have given us this bread:
fruit of the earth, work of human hands.
Blessed be God forever!

ALL: Blessed be God forever!

When all have shared the bread, the PC returns that plate to the table, picks up the plate of fruit, holds it up while saying the following blessing, eats a portion himself, then hands the plate to the person beside him.

PC:
Blessed are you,
Lord our God, Creator of the whole world,
you have made the blossoming trees
and their fruits to bring us delight.
Blessed be God forever!

ALL: Blessed be God forever!

When all have shared the fruit, the PC returns that plate to the table, picks up the cup of water, holds it up while saying the following blessing, takes a drink himself, then hands the cup to the person beside him.

PC:
Blessed are you,
Lord our God, Creator of the whole world:
you have made this water to refresh us
and to satisfy our thirst.
Blessed be God forever!

ALL: Blessed be God forever!

When all have shared the water, the PC returns that cup to the table, picks up the cup of grape juice, holds it up while saying the following blessing, takes a drink himself, then hands the cup to the person beside him.

PC:
Blessed are you,
Lord our God, Creator of the whole world:
you have given us this grape juice:
fruit of the vine, work of human hands.
Blessed be God forever!

ALL: Blessed be God forever!

When all have shared the grape juice, the PC returns that cup to the table, again opens his arms wide and says the following:)

PC:
Blessed are you, Lord our God
for all the gifts you have given your children today.
Above all we thank you for Jesus,
who lives in each of us
and for the Holy Spirit who makes us one family.
As your children,
we now join our hands and pray
as Jesus our Brother has taught us:

ALL: Our Father...

The Blessing and Peace

As soon as the Lord's Prayer is ended, the PC raises his hand in blessing.

PC:
May God's peace be with each of us here;
and may the blessing of almighty God:
the Father +, the Son, and the Holy Spirit,
come upon you all and remain with you forever.

ALL: Amen.

PC: Let us share a sign of peace with each other.

Rethinking First Communion

with Rosemary G. Conrad

Work with the RCIA has been a source of real ferment among those actively involved in American Catholic parishes. Pastors are called upon to perform a rite with the odd name of Scrutiny. Catechumenate directors must find sponsors and spiritual companions. Even the "people in the pews" find themselves asked to approve of and support "catechumens" who look very much like themselves and often live just down the street. Clearly the RCIA is making a great number of people ask questions about maturity and conversion and community.

Moreover, experiences with adults and RCIA have made many people question what Catholics have been doing with the religious formation of children. Walking with adults through their experiences of Baptism/Confirmation/Eucharist has caused many to reflect upon those sacraments as they have been celebrated with children.

A prime source of concern is over First Communion. It is clearly not just one of the sacraments of initiation but the climax of the series, yet there is some real insecurity about the customs and rituals that have grown up around it. What do they have to do with initiation? Or with Eucharist? What do Catholics really "say" to children, to parents and other relatives, and to the whole parish in the actual celebrations of First Communion?

The parish of which we are both members has had to deal with such questions just like everyone else. But there is one crucial fact about our attempts to deal with them that must be made clear: we are a small parish. There are about 450 households registered, there is no parish school, and this year we had a total of eight catechumens at Easter Vigil and sixteen children making First Communion. Obviously our attempts need to be rethought and reworked for larger parishes, but sharing the process we went through and the goals we set may help others faced with the same questions.

And so a diverse group of people—catechists, liturgists, parents, and musicians—met together one January day to brainstorm about First Communion. We began the meeting by expressing what we did *not* want the celebration in April to be.

First, we did not want a spectacle. Eucharist is not a once-for-all event like Baptism: it is repeatable. The children would not learn what it meant to be nourished at the Lord's Table amid the Lord's People by doing it once, but by doing it for a lifetime. And so we did not want "kids on parade" with special seating and elaborate decorations and flashbulbs going off and videotape cameras whirring.

(Yes, refuse to allow such equipment in church. A low-key announcement by a non-threatening person before a service is usually enough.)

Second, we did not want "cute." Our children, like everyone else's, are a little ragged around the edges. Walking in straight lines, dressing in a common uniform, reading aloud in public to adults: these are things that seven year olds don't usually do well. Nor are they part of what Eucharistic communion is all about, so we decided not to be too concerned about them.

Third, we did not want "ordinary" either. Some of our parents over the years have brought their children to the Table when they thought they were ready. And that is fine since they know how mature their children are. Yet there is a real value to making the experience special by giving it public recognition. When something important happens in our lives, sharing it with others makes the experience more real for everyone. And so we could live with "First" as a relative term.

Next, we dreamt together at our meeting about what we did want the actual celebration to be, and we came up with these three conclusions.

First, we wanted *everyone* to feel a part. Since the celebration was at a regularly scheduled Sunday Mass, we wanted the average parishioners to feel welcome. They should not have that sinking feeling inside that once again they were going to be just spectators. Instead we wanted everyone to feel that these were "our" children.

We also wanted the families to feel a part. They are the school of Christian living seven days a week, so brothers and sisters, aunts and uncles, parents and grandparents should all feel it was their day too.

And we wanted the children to feel the celebration was especially theirs. They did not need to do anything extraordinary; rather, they needed to have a share in the ordinary tasks of the Sunday assembly: processing in, preparing the gifts, exchanging peace, and so forth.

The second of the three conclusions we reached was that we wanted the service clearly related to baptism. We have experienced clearly in working with adults and the RCIA that Baptism is the "door" to the Eucharist. The children's preparation program has used Baptism as the basis for its presentations. Moreover, since we regularly celebrate Infant Baptisms at Sunday Mass, the children knew vividly what is said and done there. Now that they were old enough, we wanted to help them move a step further. We wanted to celebrate with them a "rite of passage" that would help them experience how their Baptism was being lived out in the life of their families and the larger community.

Our final conclusion was not to put all the proverbial eggs in one basket. As the RCIA with adults has taught us, a series of ceremonies allows a slow but deep growth in awareness to take place. Indeed, the Directory for Masses with Children encourages that same idea.

Various kinds of celebrations may also play a major role in the liturgical formation of children and in their preparation for the Church's liturgical life. By the very fact of celebration, children easily come to appreciate some liturgical elements, for example, greetings, silence, and common praise (Directory, 13).

And so twice, the first half of the Tuesday evening religious education meeting was an actual liturgical service. The preliminary services described in the previous chapter have proved helpful not only in the children's education but also for opening up new dimensions of prayer for the parents.

We put most of our energy, though, into developing the Sunday Eucharist. We knew when it would be—the Third Sunday of Easter. That's right: not Mother's Day or Holy Thursday or the end of the school year, but something in harmony with the flow of the liturgy. Having lived through the experiences of Holy Week and Easter with the catechumens, we now had something great to share with the children. Moreover, the Gospels of that Sunday are always about the Eucharist anyway, as are the Gospel readings for the weekdays before and after. (We sometimes seem to get so caught up in transubstantiation that we forget the point of the Scriptures: that the Jesus we meet at the Table in every Eucharist is the Risen Lord.)

On the day itself, the service began with the usual procession of the ministers, but included the children so that they would feel special. Moreover, as the Directory says, "The processional entrance of the children with the priest may help them to experience a sense of the communion that is thus constituted" (Directory, 34).

Yet when the procession reached the entrance to the sanctuary, the children went directly to where their individual families were standing in the church. Keeping the children together as a group only makes problems; having them sit with their families keeps things under control naturally. More positively, it publicly affirms the role that their relatives have played in the lives of the children and helps make everyone feel special.

The children's cathechist was the first of the readers; one of the children was the second—not to be cute but because he understood the passage and had the ability to proclaim it comprehensibly and with feeling.

After the homily, the profession of faith took the form of a renewal of baptismal promises. We kept the question-and-answer form since unison recitation of *unfamiliar* texts is not very effective and is difficult for children. But we lengthened the response ("I do" is a rather puny affirmation of faith) and tried to rewrite the questions so that they would be fully understandable to the children yet not sound childish to the adults or lapse into heresy.

After everyone had professed the faith, everyone got generously sprinkled while we all sang Carey Landry's "New Life." The point of the gesture was clear since the water was dipped up from the big baptismal pool that was still in the sanctuary from Easter Vigil. Indeed, the water continuously falling in the fountain and the six-foot-tall Easter Candle were the primary audio-visual elements in the service, and they both spoke of Baptism.

Then everyone else sat down and the children were called by name to come and stand on the sanctuary step facing the congregation. The pastor went down into the main aisle to stand by the Easter Candle and face them from the middle of the community. After recalling their Baptism, he presented each one with his or her baptismal candle (or a substitute), newly lit from the Easter Candle. He accomplished this with a little help from an acolyte: the pastor is of medium height and the Candle is big.

There were no general intercessions since the community would pray for the children during the Eucharistic Prayer; moreover, having seven year olds hold lighted candles makes them and everyone else nervous. Instead, after a triple alleluia and a big round of applause, the children took the candles back to their families and then went to the vestibule for the procession. And they came up the aisle with everything important needed for the meal: cloth and candles and bread and wine. After arranging it all with the help of the acolytes, they again returned to their families.

We used the third Eucharistic Prayer for Children with its Easter adaptation. It managed to speak to children without talking down to adults: the Easter parts of the text were appropriate, and there was a chance to do an extra few easy acclamations. We could even add a special memento for the children at the appropriate place in the Prayer.

For the Lord's Prayer, the children came up again, formed a circle around the altar, and held hands with the concelebrants while we all sang together. After the invitation to Peace, they exchanged it with each other and with others in the sanctuary before going back to share it with their families and those around.

For communion itself they had no special recognition; instead they came up with their families to the usual stations. We were strong on this point. We wanted them to come to the table in the community and with the community. As St. Paul keeps saying in 1 Corinthians, by eating and drinking we are made one with the whole Christ, with the Head and with all the members of his living Body. The traditional way of having the children come first seems to us to "individualize" that experience too much. Moreover it seems to be the point of greatest temptation for the camera enthusiasts, who destroy the actual moment of prayer in the very attempt to record it.

We invited everyone to stay for dessert on the front lawn, concluded with the Solemn Blessing for Eastertime, which speaks of us all as being God's children through Baptism, and the recessional of the ministers began—without the children.

The reactions were favorable. One immediate sign of this was that the back pews did not empty after communion even though the service was ten minutes longer than usual. The comments of families and visiting relatives during the lawn party also spoke of how they had felt so much a part of the celebration. A similar point was made by a few notes that were later received from parishioners who had no special involvement with the children.

The most important reaction came from the children. Their next Tuesday meeting was devoted to mystagogy, to help them unravel the experience. They had felt important but not on display. They had done the ordinary parts of Sunday Eucharist but in a special way. They felt now that they "belonged" (cf., Directory, 21).

Most important, though, was their reaction to Neill. A boy of twelve, handicapped from birth and in the lower-functioning level of retardation, Neill had been in our religious education program for two-and-one-half years and was ready at last for First Communion. For the last three months before the celebration he had been "mainstreamed" to a great extent into the regular program. The children learned from their teacher and from Neill what retardation is and isn't. He quickly became one of them. During the actual service he was able, with help from his relatives, to participate in everything the other children did.

During their reflections the children voiced their feeling that their first communion group was really special because Neill was one of them. This repeated remark of theirs revealed that they had learned more about communion with the living Body of Christ from Neill than from books and classes and ceremonial hoopla.

And best of all, that Sunday was Neill's thirteenth birthday.

RENEWAL OF BAPTISMAL PROMISES AT FIRST COMMUNION

After the homily this rite replaces the recitation of the Profession of Faith. It may be concelebrated by two or more presbyters or by a presbyter and deacon.

The PC and the ACC go to stand at the head of the main aisle. The children remain with their families in the pews.

The ACC/PC invites everyone to stand. The PC gives a brief introduction in his own words to the Renewal.

PC: Our faith must be in God, the all-powerful and loving maker of heaven and earth. Do you all believe in God the Father?

ALL: Yes, we believe in God the Father.

PC: Our faith must be in Jesus, God's only Son. He became human like us. He died for love of us, and he has risen again to bring us new life. Do you all believe in Jesus, God's Son?

ALL: Yes, we believe in Jesus, God's Son.

PC: Our faith must be in the Holy Spirit. By Baptism the Holy Spirit has come to live in us. He brings us together as God's family. He helps us to forgive each other and to live in love. Do you all believe in God the Holy Spirit?

ALL: Yes, we believe in God the Holy Spirit.

PC: Our faith must be in the power of the Spirit to make us the Church, the living Body of Christ. Together we eat this holy meal. Together we must serve each other and the whole world. Do you all believe in yourselves, the Church, the People of God?

ALL: Yes, we believe in ourselves, the Church, the People of God.

PC: This is our faith; this is the faith of the Church. As we profess it together today, let us relive our Baptism by which we first shared in God's own life.

An acolyte then brings over the sprinkling bowl and the branch and hands them to the ACC/PC. The ACC/PC fills the bowl from the baptismal pool, hands it back to the acolyte, and they move around all the aisles of the church, generously sprinkling the community.

Meanwhile everyone sings an appropriate song, for example, "New Life" by Carey Landry. When they have finished, the Candle Presentation ceremony follows immediately.

PRESENTATION OF BAPTISMAL CANDLES AT FIRST COMMUNION

After the sprinkling is finished, the ACC/PC invites everyone to be seated. An acolyte goes to stand by the Easter Candle with a taper. The ACC/PC then calls the children by name to come forward. Carrying their baptismal candles (or a substitute), they come forward and stand in a row on the sanctuary step, facing the congregation.

ACC/PC: Please be seated. Would the following please come forward.

He slowly reads the list of names. PC stands by candle.

PC/ACC: Dear children, when you were baptized, Jesus came to make his home in you, to fill you with the light of his resurrection. On that day your parents (and godparents) were given a candle to keep, a reminder that the risen Jesus is the light within you. Today you will share in the life of Jesus in a special way, and so we now give you the candle to keep. All of us here pray that the risen Jesus will shine within you today. We pray that you will bring his light to others: to your family and friends, to everyone you meet, today and for the rest of your lives.

The acolyte lights the taper from the Easter candle and hands it to the PC/ACC, who moves down the row of children and lights the candle of each one. He says to each:

PC/ACC: (*Name of child*), receive the light of Christ!

At the conclusion of the candle lighting, the musicians lead the community in song.

ALL: Alleluia, alleluia, alleluia!

ACC/PC: Let us welcome these boys and girls to the Table of the Lord!

He leads the community in applause, then says,

Let us now prepare for our meal with the risen Lord!

The children return to their places, give their candles to their families, and go to the vestibule for the procession with the gifts.

PART THREE:
Special Celebrations

Healing

None of us is very far from physical suffering. The child with a broken bone, the aging parent, the neighbor with MS: we are surrounded by those whose bodies are touched in some way for varying periods of time by pain. Nor is any of us exempt from this experience. Whether it be the inconvenience of the common cold or the first signs of AIDS (which has taught us again the meaning of the word "plague"), all human flesh learns the reality of suffering.

Nor is that experience merely physical. The simplest of ailments is an inward challenge. We do not have to be "into" holistic medicine to realize how the frustrations of being infirm and our anxiety about the future present a challenge to our patience with ourselves, to the charity of our relationships, and even to our faith in God. For anyone who suffers or who companions the suffering, the claim that Christian life is our individual share in Christ's passover mystery is not theological jargon but an experienced reality.

One of the (at least partially) major reforms of Vatican II was the rescue of the Anointing of the Sick from the trap into which it had fallen over the centuries. In the Roman Rite, the sacrament had first become Extreme Unction, understood not as the last of the anointings that any initiated Christian would receive but as the final departure ritual for eternity. Moreover, this delaying of the sacrament when combined with the progressive institutionalization of the sick, elderly, and dying in our culture had led to clericalized, minimalist performance. The sick were deprived of support; the community was deprived of the chance for prayerful companionship; the priest was reduced to the role of shaman; and God could work only first-class miracles.

The rite published in 1972 and revised in 1983 attempted to counteract each of these tendencies.

> This sacrament gives the grace of the Holy Spirit to those who are sick; by this grace the whole person is helped and saved, sustained by trust in God, and strengthened against the temptations of the Evil One and against anxiety over death (Pastoral Care of the Sick, 6)

Those who were *sick*, or infirm, not dying, were to be called to the sacrament (cf., esp. PCS, 13.) Since "all baptized Christians share in this ministry of mutual charity," the celebration itself was to have as much as possible a "community aspect" (PCS, 33 and 36). Priests were called not to be ritual functionaries but active participants in consoling, inspiring, and strengthening the suffering (PCS, 35). When more than one priest was present, the rite was to be concelebrated with each one laying on hands (PCS, 19). Most importantly, a rite for anointing during Mass was drawn up for the first time

(PCS #131-134). The possibility for a truly radical reorientation of this sacrament within Roman Catholic life and worship was thus created.

What has been the result after more than a decade of using this rite at Mass? Personally, I have found its structure to be simple and its style (usually) direct. If carried out with sensitivity and love yet without sentimentality by the ministers, its gestures and words can reveal amid the community the real power of the Spirit. There are, though, certain considerations that experience has shown must be taken into account.

First, the community must be primary. Just as with Infant Baptism or the RCIA, if the number of people involved in the special ceremony is reasonable, the communal worship can open up both to support and to celebrate with the suffering. In practical terms, the closer the number of those to be anointed gets to ten, the more consideration should be given to repeating the rite at two different Sunday services.

Another possibility is to involve more than one priest in concelebrating the rite. If there is no solution to the problem of numbers that are too large, then a separate Healing Mass should probably be arranged. This option runs the risk of isolating the sacrament, but the communal involvement can be maintained *if* that is a priority of the planners.

Second, no one should come to celebrate the sacrament alone. Some people need actual assistance during the rite. Yet having a "sponsor" or two by their side can be both a practical and a spiritual support for all those to be anointed. They can experience not only the total community at prayer but also the immediate commitment of family and/or friends who have come to share in the service. Having the "sponsors" lay their hands on the shoulders of the suffering (as is done in the RCIA) while the priest lays hands on the head is a warm and moving gesture. The requirements for sacramental validity are the minimum and not the optimum components of the rite.

Third, physical contact is crucial. Anyone who has ever sat by the bed of someone suffering (or who has been the one in the bed) knows how crucial it is to hold the hand or to touch the arm of the person lying there. The laying on of hands is thus as important as the anointing. Possibly supplemented by the sponsors' gesture, this moment of contact should last long enough for everyone to actually *experience* the gesture: at least one half-minute for each person.

Minimalism and legalism can quickly destroy this part of the rite. Anyone who has watched bishops confirming on the assembly line or priests laying on hands without genuine contact knows the pettiness of such gestures. Either the gesture is one of vulnerability and compassion or it is nothing. It is mechanically sufficient *that* it be done; it is spiritually essential that it be done *well*.

Fourth, each priest needs to be accompanied by an acolyte or deacon. Hopefully, the anointing formula can be memorized; but no one can juggle a jar or bowl of oil, a small towel, and possibly a card with the printed text and still perform the actual anointing with style and grace and prayer.

OUTLINE OF ANOINTING OF THE SICK WITHIN MASS

Opening Rite

Greeting - PC

Reception/Instruction - PC/ACC

Opening Prayer - PC

Celebration of the Sacrament (after the homily)

Litany - deacon/reader and musicians

Laying on of Hands - priest(s)

Blessing or Thanksgiving over the Oil - priest

Anointing - priest(s) assisted by deacon(s) and/or acolytes

Concluding Prayer - priest

Optional Additional Texts

Preface, Mementos, Final Blessing

The actual rite contains multiple options. The opening Instructions at PCS 135 is given as a model ("in these or similar words"). The following is another version based upon the instruction for the rite of anointing outside Mass at PCS 117 (or it could be used later to introduce the Litany). Though none is required, PCS 118B or C (second series) could be a brief and fitting penitential rite, or, if circumstances permit, a brief water sprinkling as a renewal of Baptism.

The Instruction

PC/ACC:
Dear friends,
we have come together here in the name of Jesus,
who often restored the sick to health
and who himself suffered so much for our sake.

Jesus is now present among us as our risen Lord.
He lives among us still
as the conqueror of sin and death.
He desires to extend the victory of his cross
in the lives of each of us
who are members of his Body.
We know that he will work through us
and will unite our prayers with his own.

Since many of our brothers and sisters here
are experiencing in some way
the weakness of our mortal bodies,
let us entrust them in Jesus' name
to the love and healing power of God our Father.

Let us (kneel and) pray!

For hospitality's sake, calling forward those to be anointed by name is effective and aids the community in prayer.

The Litany should be specially composed for each service since personal circumstances vary so markedly. At least the refrain should be sung.

An effective way of doing the laying-on of hands is to integrate it into the Litany. If one uses the final petition from PCS 138 to conclude the series, "Give life and health to our brothers and sisters, on whom we lay our hands in your name," the priest(s) can begin the actual imposition while the musicians continue to play quietly, leading the community into the repeated refrain as a kind of mantra. Or the names of those suffering can simply be read one by one between the repeated refrain.

If the number to be anointed is large and the priests must go out to their seats, consideration should be given to joining the laying-on of hands with the actual anointing. The fullness of each gesture is somewhat lessened, but the communal prayer is enhanced.

The laying-on of hands is followed either by the Blessing of Oil or a Prayer of Thanksgiving if the oil has already been blessed. Though tradition has emphasized the bishop's solemn annual consecration of the Holy Chrism and the blessing of the Oil of Catechumens and the Oil of the Sick, the roots of that practice lie in the practical need for the first two oils during the rites of initiation at Easter Vigil. It is clear from many early church orders that the Oil of the Sick was blessed more frequently as the needs of the faithful required. Episcopal blessing of the Oil of the Sick is a sign of their pastoral concern. The same criterion should be the deciding factor in whether a presbyter needs to bless more at a given service (cf., PCS 22a.)

The only real disappointment I have with the current rite is with the texts of these prayers over the oil. If the more conventional unitary prayer is chosen, the text seems a little thin to function as the climactic *public* words of the sacramental celebration. As *berakhah,* the text doesn't seem to be grand enough. Also lacking is any reference to the Litany or the imposition that have just occurred. The following is a proposal for how to take the text and open it up more (cf., PCS).

THE BLESSING OR THANKSGIVING OVER THE OIL OF THE SICK (A)

PC/ACC:
Lord, God of all consolation,
you chose and sent your Son to heal the world.
Listen in your mercy to this prayer,
which we make in faith
for those who believe in you,
on whom the elders of the Church
have laid their hands,
and who will be anointed in your name.
May they receive the health you offer
in this sacrament.

(*If the oil has been blessed:*)
At the prayer of our bishop N.N.,
you have sent the Holy Spirit, the Consoler,

(*If the oil has not been blessed:*)
Send the Holy Spirit, the Consoler,

to bless this precious oil, this soothing ointment,
this rich gift, this fruit of the earth.
By his indwelling power
may all who are anointed with this oil
be freed from every pain, illness, and disease,
and be made well again in body, mind, and soul.

Father, may this oil which you bless
for our use produce its healing effect

in the name of Jesus, our Brother and our King.
Through him you are blessed and praised
in the unity of the Holy Spirit
now and forever and ever.

ALL: (sing) Amen! Amen! Amen!

If the more litany-like prayer at PCS 140 or 140B (similar to the blessing of the water at Infant Baptism) is chosen, another difficulty arises. The community's acclamations should be sung, but the immediately preceding litany should also have a sung refrain. Moreover, the text of the blessing/prayer of thanksgiving seems to me also to need enhancement.

An alternative can be the combination of the Litany and blessing into one text. After the names of those to be anointed have been called and everyone has come forward (if possible), the PC can invite everyone to prayer:

PC:
Let us pray that God would give life
and health to our brothers and sisters
on whom we lay our hands.

The musicians can immediately begin the mantra-like repetition of the acclamation, and the priests can lay on hands. After the imposition, the PC can move behind the altar and, without a break in the background music, begin proclaiming a text like the following (cf., PCS).

THE BLESSING OVER
THE OIL OF THE SICK (B1)

The cantor sings the chosen refrain only once. The musicians continue to play quietly. A presbyter proclaims the following with the refrain repeated between each invocation.

The Invocations

ALL: (Acclamation)

PC/ACC:
Praise to you, God, the almighty Father,
You sent your Son to live among us
and bring us salvation.
Bless this oil +:
fill it with the power of your love.

ALL: (Acclamation)

PC/ACC:
Praise to you, God, the only-begotten Son.
You humbled yourself to share in our humanity,
and you heal our infirmities.
Bless this oil +;
may those anointed with it today
be given pardon and strength.

ALL: (Acclamation)

PC/ACC:
Praise to you, God, the Holy Spirit, the Consoler.
Your unfailing power gives us strength

in our bodily weakness.
Bless this oil +;
may those anointed with it today
be filled with your peace.

ALL: (Acclamation)

The Prayer

PC/ACC:
Almighty Father, come to our aid,
and by your Holy Spirit make holy this oil
which has been set apart for healing your people.
May the prayer of faith and this anointing
free them from pain, illness, and disease,
and make them whole again
in body, mind, and soul.
We ask this in the name of Jesus,
our Brother and our King.
Through him you are blessed and praised
in the unity of the Holy Spirit
now and forever and ever.

ALL: (sing) Amen! Amen! Amen!

THE THANKSGIVING OVER THE OIL OF THE SICK (B2)

The cantor sings the chosen refrain only once. The musicians continue to play quietly. A presbyter proclaims the following invocations with the refrain repeated between each.)

The Invocations

ALL: (Acclamation)

PC/ACC:
Praise to you, God, the almighty Father.
You sent your Son to live among us
and bring us salvation.
You have blessed this oil;
fill it now with the power of your love.

ALL: (Acclamation)

PC/ACC:
Praise to you, God, the only-begotten Son.
You humbled yourself to share in our humanity,
and you heal our infirmities.
You have blessed this oil;
may those anointed with it today
be given pardon and strength.

ALL: (Acclamation)

PC/ACC:
Praise to you, God, the Holy Spirit, the Consoler.
Your unfailing power gives us strength

in our bodily weakness.
You have blessed this oil;
may those anointed with it today
be filled with your peace.

ALL: (Acclamation)

The Prayer

PC/ACC:
Almighty Father,
at the prayer of our bishop N.N.,
your Holy Spirit has made holy this oil
which has been set apart for healing your people.
May the prayer of faith and this anointing
free them from pain, illness, and disease,
and make them whole again
in body, mind, and soul.
We ask this in the name of Jesus,
our Brother and our King.
Through him you are blessed and praised
in the unity of the Holy Spirit
now and forever and ever.

ALL: (sing) Amen! Amen! Amen!

The concluding prayer after the anointing has four options, not all of which are suitable for a public service. Given the importance of communal support and physical contact, cannot the Exchange of Peace be substituted? After the last person is anointed and the priests have cleaned their hands, a deacon or presbyter can invite the community to stand; a priest can proclaim the usual Prayer for Peace; or the invitation to the exchange can be given and everyone can move around for a while. The intensity of the overall service will then be broken in a healthy way before everyone gathers back together again for the Eucharistic Prayer and the Holy Meal.

Again, as with Infant Baptism, there is no need to try to make the rest of the service all that special. The decorations, readers, and distributors, the other texts of the service should be what the community expects and can claim as their own. Those anointed or their "sponsors" might make the presentation of the gifts. The powerful new preface at PCS 143 may be proclaimed (if the seasonal celebration allows it); at least the special memento for the sick found there should be used. The final blessing should be one of those given at PCS 147, unless a seasonal one would be more appropriate. Yet there is no need to focus too much on those anointed during the rest of the service; the whole community needs to surrender themselves to God in prayer and praise.

In addition to the sacrament of Anointing of the Sick, a widespread practice of prayer for healing of all types has been growing in the American Catholic Church. Some people feel themselves called by the Spirit to undertake healing as a personal ministry, a call and a gift that needs to be respected. In other circumstances the focus is upon the common prayer of the assembled Body of Christ for the wholeness of the members.

The following service is an attempt to give liturgical expression to the second type of focus. I have participated only occasionally in this service but have found the experiences prayerful. Scheduled for a Sunday Eucharist in Ordinary Time when the readings were appropriate, the rite was effective because the community had been prepared with a clearer understanding of the rite for two weeks in advance through announcements. They seemed therefore comfortable entering not only into the verbal components but even into the physical contact, which can be a threatening part of the rite.

A HEALING SERVICE DURING EUCHARIST

An attractive jar containing an appropriate amount of oil, which might be slightly scented, stands upon the altar in plain view. A sufficient number of small bowls or cups rests along either side, or else those who are to help distribute the oil already have them in their possession. The credence table is so arranged that the bowls can later be placed there.

After the Homily everyone sits for a few minutes in reflection. A presbyter then goes to stand behind the altar and face the congregation. Everyone remains seated. The rite may be concelebrated.

The Blessing

PC:
Let us pray in our hearts
that God will heal each one of us today/tonight.

(*Pause*)

Lord God, loving Father,
to the sick and the poor
your Son Jesus brought healing and peace.
To the outcast and the broken
he brought the hope of new life,
restoring once again their dignity and salvation.

As we call upon you now in faith,
send your Holy Spirit upon us once more.

Let us experience anew your compassion.
And, Father, bless this oil +;
make it a sign of your healing and forgiveness.
May all who are touched by it
today/tonight be made whole again
in mind and body, in heart and spirit.

We make this prayer in the name of Jesus
and by the power of the Spirit within us.
Glory and praise be yours now and forever!

ALL: (sing) Amen!

The Anointing

*A deacon or the presbyter who has blessed the oil
pours a portion of the oil into each bowl and marks
the forehead of each distributor with the oil before
handing him or her the bowl, or else pours it into the
bowl that the distributor brings up and then marks
his or her forehead. As each distributor receives his
or her bowl, each one immediately goes to his or her
assigned portion of the community and begins to
mark the forehead of the first person, who then
marks the second person, and so on.*

*As each person marks someone else's forehead
with the oil in the form of a cross, he or she says:*

May the Lord Jesus heal you!

*Each distributor is responsible for returning his
or her bowl to the credence table.*

The General Intercessions

When everyone has been anointed and everything is calm again, a presbyter begins the Intercessions.

PRESBYTER: Let us stand and pray!

The cantor sings the refrain through only once. An acolyte goes to the lectern to proclaim the intentions.

Jesus, you came that we might have life, and have it to the full:

For all who seek your guidance, be the Good Shepherd:

To all who are lonely, anxious, or depressed, give your peace:

Mend broken relationships, and break open our stubborn hearts:

Remove old bitterness, and set us free.

Whatever our sinfulness has broken, restore now to wholeness:

Give strength to the sick, the injured, to all we remember today/tonight:

Other suitable petitions may be added, or some of those above may be omitted. The concluding intention is always the following:

Hear us, O Lord of life; heal us all, and make us whole:

The presbyter says the Concluding Prayer, and the Presentation of the Gifts begins immediately. The jar of oil is removed from the altar now if it had not been before.

The Blessing is an adaptation from the sacramental rite; the General Intercessions are adapted from the Episcopalian *Book of Occasional Services*. These components might be rearranged. During a retreat I participated in, this service was combined with Vespers. After the psalmody, the reading was an appropriate Gospel selection. After a brief homily, the blessing and anointing took place. Vespers then continued with the Canticle of Mary and the litany given above as the Intercessions. In the quiet of evening with the fragrant incense lifting our praise to God, who "looks upon (our) lowliness," I experienced a real sense of renewal.

And that experience is part of my heritage as a Christian. In the resurrection of Jesus, "death has been swallowed up in victory," as Paul says in Corinthians 1. The infirmities of our flesh, the brokenness of our hearts, the pains we all feel in body and spirit: these have all lost their power to enslave us. It is an essential part of our baptismal vocation to proclaim and to act out in prayer and ritual the healing power of the Good News. By our faith and hope, our patience and love, the reality of the new creation will be revealed bit by bit, day after day, slowly yet surely.

> The one sitting on the throne spoke: Look, I am making the whole of creation new....What I am saying is sure and will come true (Rev. 21, 5 JB).

Matrimony

Around 1973 I experienced an odd sequence of events that still colors my outlook. In one year I attended eight funerals; the next year, eight weddings. Either could have produced ritual burnout; their juxtaposition forced me to certain observations.

The funerals, though usually arranged in a short time, were more spontaneous and prayerful, more genuine and inviting experiences than the weddings. Some of the deaths were unexpected or tragic, but repeatedly those gathered for the service rose above their grief to celebrate the promise of faith. Admittedly, the weddings occurred in the heyday of *The Velveteen Rabbit* and Kahlil Gibran (or Gibbering Kahlil as I nicknamed him); yet they seemed flat and inauthentic by contrast. Not until the reception did the robust good humor natural to the occasion usually break forth.

I have since been to many enjoyable weddings, especially those celebrated within a strong ethnic tradition. But my first reaction to another invitation in the mailbox is still a sinking feeling and a quiet urge to fabricate an excuse for cutting the ceremony while showing up for the reception. Maybe my outlook is a little too "incarnational"; but many Western medieval marriage orders concluded with an epithalamion (blessing of the marriage bed), while the nuptial blessings prayed for health, wealth, happiness, and friends and children to rejoin the party in the new and eternal Jerusalem.

Perhaps we can do little to end the privatization and romanticization with which contemporary American culture surrounds marriage, but as Roman Catholics we have a tradition that could provide alternatives. I think of the alternatives as process, community, and adaptation.

Process

Roman Catholics have been learning from the RCIA (and hopefully soon from the Order of Christian Funerals) how crucial the element of process is in psychological and spiritual development. Prospective new Roman Catholics need not only to be instructed in doctrine and morality but to be integrated into the life of prayer and service within the local parish. Step by step they move gradually into a new identity and a new way of living. Those grieving also need more than just personal cards and a nice "memorial service." Instead they need the rhythm of vigil, funeral, and committal as they explore the new identity and lifestyle that loss has given them.

In a similar way, the engaged should have ritual milestones as they move toward the wedding. Pre-Cana, Engaged Encounter, and other marriage preparation programs fill certain needs well, but the engaged still need public recognition of their new status and the prayerful support of the faith community.

One way of providing such a communal ritual would be a periodic blessing for engaged couples. In contemporary America the actual engagement should not be a religious event. Yet blessing and prayer for crucial moments in life is something Christians should ask of their community.

The practicality of such a blessing would vary widely. In a smaller or more tightly-knit parish, such a practice would be natural. In a larger or urban parish, more catechesis and preparation would be necessary. In an age, though, when people are mobile, some attempt at such a blessing would help congregations have some ritual share in the wedding process.

Such a blessing could also be the climax of a prayer service at a wedding preparation program or, if the parents felt up to it, as part of a family gathering. Whatever the setting, a sense of process and a need for community call for some attempt at public prayer.

Another option is to integrate such a blessing into the announcements and last blessing of Sunday Eucharist. Such a blessing could take the form of a presidential *berakhah* or perhaps a four-part solemn blessing. To succeed, it needs a presider who can be warm in welcome and convincing at prayer. The communal applause and presidential gesture are as important as the words.

A BLESSING
FOR ENGAGED COUPLES (A)

This rite is not an engagement ritual but rather a blessing to be given within a church assembly to those couples who have been recently engaged. An especially appropriate time would be during Sunday Eucharist.

This rite may be led by either a presbyter or deacon; it may also be concelebrated.

The Introduction

After postcommunion, the announcements are made as usual. Then an appropriate person stands at the lectern and invites each couple to come forward while he or she introduces their names and gives a little information about each. (An appropriate person would be whoever directs the parish premarital instruction program, an individual or couple who works in that program, or a member of the pastoral staff.)

The couples stand at the step into the sanctuary, facing the congregation. When all have been introduced, the PC leads the community in applause.

The Invitation

PC/ACC: I invite all the engaged couples to join hands; and I ask us all to bow our heads and pray in our hearts for God to bless these couples during their engagement.

The Blessing

The PC or ACC lifts his hand in blessing and prays:

PC/ACC:
We thank you,
God of all goodness, source of all love.
In the beginning
you created us in your own image:
male and female you created us—
that we might share in the mystery of love.,
that the world might be drawn back into unity.
And when we were broken and divided,
your Son Jesus died on the cross
to reveal how deep love must be.

We thank you today
for these engaged couples gathered here.
They have begun to discover
the mystery of love in each other:
bless them + as they grow in that love.
Help them by prayer and discernment
to be honest with themselves and with each other.
Let their affection grow into deep human care,
their attraction into lasting commitment.
May they find ever greater delight
in each other's company.
Fill them with your Holy Spirit
that in the mystery of human love
they may find the presence and power
of the divine.

This we ask in the name of Jesus
and by the power of the Spirit moving us to pray.
Glory and honor be yours forever and ever.

ALL: (sing or say) Amen!

The Blessing and Dismissal

PC: And may almighty God bless you all:
the Father, the Son +, and the Holy Spirit.

ALL: Amen!

ACC/PC: The Mass is ended. Go in peace!

ALL: Thanks be to God!

The engaged couples return to their places, and the recessional goes by as usual.

A BLESSING FOR ENGAGED COUPLES (B)

This rite is not an engagement ritual but rather a blessing to be given within a church assembly to those couples who have been recently engaged. An especially appropriate time would be during Sunday Eucharist.

This rite may be led by either a presbyter or deacon; it may also be concelebrated.

The Introduction

After postcommunion, the announcements are made as usual. Then an appropriate person stands at the lectern and invites each couple to come forward while he or she introduces their names and gives a little information about each. (An appropriate person would be whoever directs the parish premarital instruction program, an individual or couple who works in that program, or a member of the pastoral staff.)

The couples stand at the step into the sanctuary, facing the congregation. When all have been introduced, the PC leads the community in applause.

The Invitation

PC/ACC: I invite all the engaged couples to join hands; and I ask us all to bow our heads and pray in our hearts for God to bless these couples during their engagement.

The Blessing

He pauses, then lifts his hands in blessing.

Father, these engaged couples
have begun to discover
the mystery of love in each other.
Bless them as they grow in that love.

ALL: Amen!

PC/ACC:
Help them be honest in their discernment.
Let their affection grow into deep human care,
their attraction into lasting commitment.

ALL: Amen!

PC/ACC:
Fill them with your Holy Spirit
that in the mystery of human love
they many find the presence and power
of the divine.

ALL: Amen!

PC:
And may almighty God bless you all:
the Father, the Son +, and the Holy Spirit.

ALL: Amen!

The Blessing and Dismissal

PC: And may Almighty God bless you all:
the Father, the Son, and the Holy Spirit.

ALL: Amen!

ACC/PC: The Mass is ended. Go in peace!

ALL: Thanks be to God!

The engaged couples return to their places, and the recessional goes by as usual.

Another possible preliminary ritual could be the blessing of the wedding rings at the rehearsal rather than at the wedding itself. Preliminary blessings of objects is a frequent practice in the Roman Rite (such as at the Easter Vigil). Many rehearsals already include a few moments of prayer; adding such a blessing could add a concrete focus and ritual to the experience. Other bits of ritual such as the visit to the Mary shrine or even the candle lighting so frequently seen could be incorporated into the rehearsal. Such semi-public services with their increased intimacy often allow certain gestures to speak with much more power than they would in a larger context.

Community

The wedding service requires the active participation of the community if it is to be an experience and not a show. Yet such a statement runs utterly counter to the prevailing American ethos. One Presbyterian friend of mine occasionally complains about Catholic weddings because of "all the popping up and down" while things go on and on. He expects to go to church to *watch* the service with no greater external participation than bowing his head for prayer and whispering an Amen. Unfortunately, many practicing Roman Catholics exhibit the same reticence even though they participate weekly in the Eucharist.

The only antidote to this attitude is to face it. No one should be upbraided or made to feel guilty; instead some form of hospitable welcome is necessary. Just before the opening procession, someone—

family member, staff person, clergy, whoever can be warm and inviting—should address the congregation. This welcome should help strangers feel at home with participation aids, gestures, postures, and with the restrictions on sharing in communion. If people feel comfortable and are specifically invited to share in the service, they will.

Adaptation

The most showy part of the typical wedding, the parade down the main aisle, is not even in the official liturgy. Beyond pointing out to couples that what they have seen elsewhere is not what they have to do, I know of no effective way to downplay this custom. The only effective version I have known is the participation of the wedding party with the liturgical ministers in the opening procession, with the bride and groom each accompanied by both parents.

The service itself lacks coherence and dramatic flow. Just as with Infant Baptism, the individual components are all sound, but their structure is deficient. Primary and secondary elements run into each other or are kept separate but equal. The most obvious incoherences are the elements surrounding the exchange of vows and the delay of the nuptial blessing until after the Lord's Prayer (a meaningless archaism). The format used in the *Book of Common Prayer* and the recently approved ecumenical liturgy suggest a possible rearrangement.

The following proposal could retain the Roman Rite's words almost intact and in almost the existing order but redistributed within the service.

The Opening Rite

Procession

Instruction
> Addressed to the community as well as to the couple.

Declaration of Consent
> Including an optional question addressed to the community.

Opening Prayer

Moving the instruction and declaration of consent to the beginning fills in an obvious gap where the procession normally does not lead up to any significant opening words or gesture (the penitential rite?). Moreover, separating the questions from the vows eliminates a seeming repetition. The community is also drawn into the service in a more natural way if addressed in the beginning and asked also to make some sort of commitment. The collective prayer and the Word flow naturally out of such an opening.

The following is a proposal to adapt the Instruction to fit this rearrangement (cf., Rite of Matrimony 58).

The Instruction

PC/ACC:
My dear friends,

we have all come together in this church
so that the Lord may seal and strengthen
the love of NN. and NN.
in the presence of the Church's minister(s)
and of this whole community.
Christ abundantly blesses this love.
He has already consecrated this couple
in Baptism.
Now he enriches and strengthens them
by a special sacrament
so that they may assume the duties of marriage
in mutual and lasting fidelity.

(*Addressing the couple,*)
And so, in the presence of the Church,
I ask you, NN. and NN., to state your intentions.

The Wedding

Exchange of Vows

(Blessing and) Exchange of Rings

Receiving of the Vows

Nuptial Blessing

(Exchange of Peace)

(General Intercessions)

If the presbyter or deacon stands amid the assembly for the exchange of vows, it strengthens everyone's common role as witness, and the couple becomes visible for the heart of the service. The vows are thus verbally and visually the climax of the rite. To maintain this flow, the rings should be exchanged *before* the receiving of the vows, as the first and—in our culture—the most crucial of the explanatory rites. (As described above, the rings might be blessed previously.)

The Episcopalian and ecumenical services make this clear even in the formula of reception.

> Now that A and B have given themselves to each other by solemn vows, with the joining of hands and the giving and receiving of rings, I announce to you that they are husband and wife. Those whom God has joined together let no one put asunder.

The two traditional elements of equal importance to the *sacrament* of Matrimony are the couple's vows and the church's blessing (c.f., Kenneth Stevenson's *Nuptial Blessing*). Since there is no reason to maintain any separation between these two, the presbyter or deacon should step back up to preside over this part of the service.

Gesture is once again crucial. The presider speaks the words, but the whole community is at prayer. His invitation to stand and pray must therefore be open and embracing. Involving the parents and wedding party in the laying on of hands also opens up the gesture. Inviting everyone to extend their hands opens it even further. As at Confirmation, the legal requirements for validity state the minimum and not the optimum.

At the end of the nuptial blessing, applause would be the natural concomitant to the concluding Amen. Since in many places it is customary for the bride and groom to greet their parents then, could not the exchange of peace be moved to this point to dignify the gesture and to deepen its meaning?

The general intercessions seem unnecessary because there are so many other intercessory elements in the total ceremony. If they are included, their universal focus means that they are more appropriate after rather than before the nuptial blessing (and exchange of peace). In fact, the couple should probably not even be mentioned among the intentions.

More Rites

Just as at Baptism and Orders there are additional objects and gestures to help make the richness of the sacrament more evident, so other explanatory rites for Matrimony have developed in various cultures. As mentioned before, the exchange of rings is the primary symbol in contemporary America. Some ethnic traditions have their own. I have seen, for instance, the Latin American woven braid hung around the couple's shoulders.

One of the most popular rites is the candle-lighting ceremony, in which the couple, each holding a lighted taper, together light a third taper and then extinguish their own. It is a simple ceremony that needs *no* additional words and could have a place in the rite after the receiving of the vows and before the nuptial blessing.

Another explanatory rite is the wrapping of the couple's joined hands in the priest or deacon's stole during the reception of the vows. If this "tying of the knot" helps make clear the presence of God in married love and the indissolubility of marriage, the gesture seems appropriate. If it is experienced as clericalism, then problems arise. Perhaps if the presider were simply to lay a hand on the couple's joined hands, the gesture might be just as clear.

Another custom has been the visit to the shrine of the Blessed Mother. I hesitate to call this an explanatory rite since it is a devotional practice with no connection to Matrimony. Especially given the changing patterns of Catholic piety, the practice often seems inauthentic, especially when accompanied by a syrupy hymn from the 1940s or '50s. Moreover, if only the bride makes the visit, an odd message seems to be communicated. Invoking the saints is a custom to be cherished; yet the specifics of this rite are in great need of reconsider-ation.

There are other liturgical resources that need to be explored, such as the two alternative nuptial blessings in the appendix of the Roman Rite. The French and other national conferences have composed more of their own—a practice that the Roman document itself encourages (cf. RM 12-18). There is also a proper *Hanc igitur* when Eucharistic Prayer I is proclaimed; proper mementos for the other Eucharistic Prayers can easily be composed. The final blessings can be simplified and adapted.

Every generation must adapt its heritage to new circumstances and new insights. Roman Catholics in this country are no exception. Our rich sacramental tradition can provide us with a wide range of resources for celebrating Matrimony in a way that is both forceful and contemporary. Without adopting wholesale the customs of our surrounding culture, we can create services that truly proclaim the joy and vitality of Christian marriage. Through process and community involvement, we can develop a ritual that will lead the couple, their families, and the parish more deeply into God's dynamic love still at work among us.

Jubilee and Renewal of Religious Profession

Now with all our heart we follow you;
we reverence you and seek your presence.
Lord, fulfill our hope
(Consecration to a Life of Virginity 41).

Each religious community has its own traditions for the celebration of profession of vows, usually within the context of a community Eucharist. Yet the anniversaries of profession are often celebrated within a parish where the religious has some personal involvement. Such services can be joyous events in which the religious and the parish re-affirm and proclaim their common life in God. I have also been at some that could only be described as self-canonizations, in which Sister took over the communal worship for that Sunday with her favorite music, or Father preached about himself and not about the Scriptures.

Reflecting upon such diverse experiences, I would say that the crucial difference lay in the underlying ecclesiology at work. Was the parish community there to be spectators and audience as at so many weddings; or were we called to be the primary liturgical actor acclaiming, affirming, ratifying, as in good RCIA celebrations? Was the ritual founded upon the common call of Baptism or on some elitist theology of religious life? Were we there to watch someone else have an experience, or were we there to have one ourselves?

The first ingredient for a successful jubilee as part of a parish's Sunday worship is, paradoxically, "ordinariness." The parish community should recognize and own its worship for that Sunday. Just as with Infant Baptism or First Communion, there must be an awareness of and a solid respect for an "average" parishioner who has just walked in on something and needs to be brought into the celebration.

A certain restraint in decorations, using the sacramentary and lectionary selections as givens, building the music around the Scriptures: all those elements that say this is what we usually do are crucial. Hospitality would make including special guests as readers or distributors appropriate, but the complete substitution of strangers for parishioners in these ministries is disruptive, especially if they can't function effectively in unfamiliar surrounding. Special events do not have to dominate an entire service; the liturgy belongs to the people, not to the planners.

The second ingredient for success is active inclusion of the assembly in the renewal of vows. Religious profession is a call to live our common Baptism in a specific lifestyle; religious life, especially within a noncontemplative order, is meant to bear witness to certain Gospel values amid our common service to the Church. Situating the renewal of religious profession within the context of a communal renewal of baptismal promises is the appropriate ritual element to reveal that common call.

The following service attempts to achieve that kind of integration. Originally based on the final vows of a Jesuit friend, it has since been adapted for the jubilees of other religious orders. Its baptismal element can be emphasized by sprinkling everyone with blessed water during the Profession of Faith, but that gesture is not necessary since there are other nonverbal elements in the service: the laying-on of hands and the Exchange of Peace.

A third ingredient in constructing the service is successfully blending the roles of the religious superior and of the priest. The superior is there to call for and to receive the profession in the name of a given religious community; the priest is there to receive and bless the profession in the name of the whole Church. Where the superior is also ordained a priest, the roles may be united, but that is still not necessary. A graceful "concelebration" of this rite is an effective sign of the meaning of religious life within the context of the believing community.

Explanatory rites are also sometimes used. Just as with the anointing and the presentation of robes and candles at Baptism, so these are intended to unfold the richness of the event. Yet a certain restraint and an awareness of good ritual is appropriate here. After ten years I have not forgotten one profession in which the superior picked up a candle lying on the altar, lit it at one of the altar candles, and handed it to the young religious with the words, "As sign and symbol of your dedication to Christ, receive this lighted candle." Unfortunately, the young woman had to blow it out immediately to exchange the peace. I hoped that this was not to be an omen of her stay in religious life.

More importantly, the words were theologically inept. I could picture the deacon entering the darkened church at Easter Vigil, singing, "Sign and symbol of Christ our Light!" or a distributor handing over the cup with the words, "Sign and symbol of the Blood of Christ." If explanatory rites are used, they must be strong both in gesture and in words done with conviction. (I would even change the formula for the exchange of rings at marriage from "Take and wear this ring as a sign of my love and fidelity" to "Take and wear this ring and remember my love and fidelity.") In a sense the Exchange of Peace is the most effective explanation of this rite (cf., Consecration of a Life of Virginity 70).

The General Intercessions are not necessary, especially if a special memento for the jubilarian and all religious is added to the Eucharistic Prayer. A suitable solemn blessing can conclude the service, but no other special elements are needed. The rhythm and joy that should be part of any Sunday Eucharist can carry everyone along as we ponder and thank God again for the diversity and the unity of the gifts that the Spirit has lavished upon the Church.

A RITE FOR
RENEWING RELIGIOUS PROFESSION

After the homily a concelebrating presbyter (CC) and the religious superior (RS) come to the head of the main aisle. The community remains seated. The RS calls by name those renewing profession forward.

RS: Would those renewing religious profession please come forward.

The Invitation to the Jubilarian

When they have all come forward and are standing in a row facing the RS and CC, the RS addresses them in these or similar words.

RS: N. and N., of your own free will you have come here in response to the call of your superiors spoken in the name of the (*name of religious order*).

Through many years you have been tested and have grown in experience and faith. You have shared in our community and our ministry.

You have come to recognize yourself as a (*name of order*), as one who is a sinner, yet called to be a companion of Jesus for the building of the kingdom.

You desire now to renew your incorporation into (*name of order*).

As the prelude to your renewed profession of religious vows, I invite you to profess the Catholic faith together with your (*name of order*) brothers/sisters and this entire community.

Renew with us the vows of Baptism, and with a courageous heart proclaim your faith in Christ, our crucified and risen Lord.

The Invitation to the Community and Profession of Faith
The CC addresses everyone in these or similar words.

CC: As we join with N. and N./those who are committing themselves again to Christ, let us stand and renew our own baptismal covenant.

ALL: We believe in one God...

The CC may sprinkle the community with blessed water during the recitation of the Profession of Faith.

The Renewal of Religious Vows
When the Creed is finished, the RS addresses those renewing their profession.

RS: N. and N., in Baptism you have already died to sin and been consecrated by the Spirit to God's service.

Now I ask you to profess your intention to continue living that Baptism in a life of apostolic service in religious community for the rest of your days.

JUBILARIANS: *(one at a time repeat the short vow formula)*

RS: N. and N., I receive your vows with joy in the name of the *(name of order)* and of the whole Church.

ALL: Alleluia! Alleluia! Alleluia! *(or in Lent another suitable acclamation).*

Prayer for the Professed

The General Intercessions may follow. At their conclusion, the CC addresses the community.

CC: Please (stand,) extend your right hands, and pray!

The CC lays both hands on the head of each jubilarian, pausing for some time. The RS accompanies him and lays his/her hand on the shoulder of each jubilarian. Meanwhile the whole community sings an appropriate refrain several times, e.g., "Come, Holy Spirit."
The CC then steps back and prays:

Almighty Father,
look with favor on these men/women
who have now reaffirmed their commitment
to follow Christ and to serve in his name

within the (*name of order*).
Give them courage, patience, and vision.
Do not let them settle down in comfort,
but give them the spirit of
(*name of founder of order*).
And strengthen us all in our Christian vocation
of witness to the world and of service to others.
May your Spirit pour out his gifts upon all
and bring us at last to the fullness of life
in your kingdom. Grant what we ask through
Christ our Lord.

ALL: (sing) Amen! Amen! Amen!

CC leads everyone in applause.

The Exchange of Peace

CC:
The Lord Jesus said,
"Peace is my farewell to you;
peace is my gift to you."
This is the bond that unites the whole Church;
this is his promise today and till the end of time.
May the peace of the Lord be always with you!

ALL: And also with you.

CC: In love and support, let us exchange Christ's
peace with N. and N./these jubilarians and all our
sisters and brothers.

The Instruction before Eucharist

CC: (*to the community*) With all our heart let us follow Christ; let us seek his presence in this Eucharist as once again he leads us back to our loving Father.

The jubilarians go to make the presentation of the gifts.

Index

Save Time and Energy With

Use these creative ideas to refresh your liturgical planning!

Symbols for All Seasons: *Planning Worship Environments for Cycles A, B, and C* by Catherine H. Krier. Is planning your church's worship environment Sunday after Sunday exhausting both your time and your supply of ideas? If so, then you need this book, which is chock-full of symbols based on the Sunday lectionary readings of all three cycles. Each entry includes space for you to jot down your own ideas. Additionally, you'll not only find key symbols to assist your planning, you'll get tips on liturgy planning, artistic considerations, and color.
Paperbound, $9.95, ISBN 0-89390-121-0

The Modern Liturgy Planning Guide by Robert Zappulla et al. A great planning resource for liturgists! You'll receive a Scripture commentary, idea starters, and music suggestions for every Sunday of Cycles A, B, and C of the Roman lectionary — along with seasonal comments and suggestions in a workbook format so that you can retain your notes for the next cycle.
Paperbound, $19.95, ISBN 0-89390-088-5

In The Potter's Hand by Robert Eimer O.M.I. and Sarah O'Malley O.S.B. These scripture-based wake services provide more flexibility, broader choices, and greater personalization, which allow bereaved family members to get more out of the service. Each service centers around a symbol, and that symbol is reflected in the readings, psalms, and prayers. You can also choose your service according to the season of the year, and either use them as is or with your own variations. Please write to Resource Publications for information on bulk prices.
Paperbound, $6.95, ISBN 0-89390-132-6

The Holy Week Book edited by Eileen E. Freeman. Plan more creative Holy Week liturgies with this important resource. It provides historical background, liturgical theology, creative ideas, and more than 60 practical presentations on Palm Sunday, Holy Thursday, Good Friday, and the Easter Vigil. Includes: Palm Sunday parade, Passover seder ideas, build-it-yourself cross for Good Friday, children's celebrations, and decorating ideas.
Paperbound, $19.95, ISBN 0-89390-007-9

The Word and Eucharist Handbook by Lawrence J. Johnson. A reference guide to the Liturgy of the Word and the Liturgy of the Eucharist. Designed especially for worship planners, ministers, and liturgical artists, use it to answer your questions about the origin, development, and modern practice of each part of the Mass.
Paperbound, $9.95, ISBN 0-89390-067-2

These Planning Resources

Come, Let Us Celebrate! *Creative Reconciliation Services* by Robert Eimer, OMI, and Sarah O'Malley, OSB. These sixteen services are adaptable for Rites II and III of the Roman Catholic sacrament of penance. They have been tried out in a parish setting and are easy to re-create. Each has symbols and themes carried out in the prayers, homily, examination, scripture readings, and songs. The book also includes twelve ideas that can be used to create additional services. Paperbound, $9.95, ISBN 0-89390-082-6

ORDER FORM

Order these books from your local religious bookstore, or complete this order form and mail it to:

Resource Publications, Inc.
160 E. Virginia St., Suite 290
San Jose, CA 95112-5848
Or call (408) 286-8505.

QTY	TITLE	PRICE	TOTAL
_____	Symbols For All Seasons	$ 9.95	_____
_____	The Modern Liturgy Planning Guide	$19.95	_____
_____	The Word And Eucharist Handbook	$ 9.95	_____
_____	In The Potter's Hand	$ 6.95	_____
_____	The Holy Week Book	$19.95	_____
_____	Come, Let Us Celebrate!	$ 9.95	_____

Subtotal: _____

*Postage and Handling: _____

California residents add 6% sales tax: _____

Total amount: _____

*Postage and Handling:
$1.50 for orders under $10.00
$2.00 for orders of $10.00 to $25.00
9% (max. $7.00) of order for orders over $25.00

[ ] My check or money order is enclosed.
[ ] Charge my [ ] VISA [ ] MC   Expire date _____

Card No. _____-_____-_____-_____

Signature _____

Name _____

Institution _____

Street _____

City _____ St _____ Zip _____